'This is inspired publishing, not only archivally valuable, but capable of bringing the past back to life without the usual filter of academic or biographer.' *Guardian*

'Intriguing insight into political background to conflict.' Customer review [on *War in the Falklands, 1982*]

'Tim Coates' brilliant new book ... uses original FBI files to recreate the period.' *Daily Express* [on *John Lennon: the FBI files*]

'Like Samuel Pepys, Denning ... took obvious pleasure in the English language. His canny, wry and at times indignant observations make this official report of a board of inquiry a wonderful entertaining and extraordinary read.... The writing is superb and the photojournalism is just as revealing.' *The Age* (Victoria, Australia) [on *The Scandal of Christine Keeler and John Profumo: Lord Denning's Report, 1963*]

'These volumes are monuments to the maligned bureaucratic architects who shaped our contemporary world – in part chilling, in part inspiring.... They show the search for order and sense amid the chaos of events, the debris of crime or the aftermath of disaster.' *Times Higher Education Supplement*

# THE HUTTON INQUIRY, 2003–4

'The best stories have been told a hundred times. They have been revisited by historians, adapted by novelists, travestied by film-makers, recycled by TV producers. None of those versions, however, can avoid the distorting wisdom of hindsight. For this reason if no other, the appearance of ...[this] series of official reports ... should be greeted with cries of joy.' *Financial Times*

'We congratulate you for the beauty and the value of the books shown.' Professor Dr Ionel Oprisan, *Editura Saeculum,* Romania, on *The Irish Book of Death and Flying Ships*

'A rare insight into the catastrophic Gallipoli campaign.' *Worcester Evening News* [on *Lord Kitchener and Winston Churchill*]

'There is a clarity that resonates down the years and it is because of this that [the books] have considerable appeal.... The events, although described in the cold official prose of senior military and political figures, nevertheless retain a freshness and immediacy.' *Worcester Evening News* [on *British Battles of World War I*]

'This is raw history.... To counter the polite but insistent letters of the British are translated speeches by the Führer, showing what his true intentions were. It's particularly satisfying to see Goering getting a dressing down from a British diplomat.' *Military Weekly* [on *War 1939*]

# THE HUTTON INQUIRY, 2003–4

*Extracts from the report which appeared on the Hutton Inquiry Website on 28 January 2004*

## SERIES EDITOR: TIM COATES

London and New York

Applications for reproduction should be made in writing to Tim Coates, c/o Littlehampton Book Services, Durrington, West Sussex BN13 3RB, UK or c/o Midpoint Trade Books, 27 West 20th Street, Suite 1102, New York, NY 10011, USA.

ISBN 1843810298

A CIP catalogue record for this book is available from the British Library.

Editor: Frances Maher
Design: Sarah Theodosiou
Printed in the United Kingdom by Cox and Wyman
Series Editor: Tim Coates

Australian edition published in association with Australian Publishing Pty Ltd, Suite 102, 282 Collins Street, Melbourne, Victoria 3000. Tel: 03 9654 0250 Fax: 03 0663 0161

Cover photograph © Rex Features/Nils Jorgensen: British Prime Minister Tony Blair in Downing Street, April 2003

Editor's note

The intention of this brief compilation from Lord Hutton's report was to provide a reader with something more than can be written in newspapers following a publication of this kind. It was prepared in haste and for the errors that has produced I apologise.

It ought to be the intention that such events as are described should never happen again. The tragedy for Dr Kelly and his family is overwhelming.

Tim Coates, January 2004

On 24 September 2002 the British Labour government published a dossier on Iraq's weapons of mass destruction which included the statement that Saddam Hussein's military planning allowed for some of those weapons to be ready within 45 minutes of an order to use them.

On 18 March 2003 British Prime Minister Tony Blair won House of Commons backing to send UK forces into battle with Saddam Hussein, and the US-led campaign to topple the Iraqi leader began two days later, shortly after US President George Bush's deadline for Saddam Hussein to go into exile or face war had expired.

On 29 May 2003 a BBC reporter announced that he had been told by 'one of the senior officials in charge of drawing up the September dossier that the government probably knew the 45-minute figure was wrong even before it decided to put it in' and that 'Downing Street a week before publication ordered it to be sexed up to be made more exciting and ordered more facts to be discovered'.

On 17 July 2003 a British scientist and expert in chemical and biological warfare, who was employed by the government to advise it on weapons in such warfare, left his Oxfordshire home and did not return. His body was found the following day.

The British government appointed Lord Hutton – previously known for his role in the extradition case against General Augusto Pinochet of Chile – 'urgently to conduct an investigation into the circumstances surrounding the death of Dr David Kelly', which occurred two days after he appeared before the Foreign Affairs Select Committee of the House of Commons and one day after he gave evidence before the Intelligence and Security Committee.

On 21 July 2003 Lord Hutton made a statement on the range and nature of the investigation. He said that the government had promised to provide him 'with the fullest cooperation and that it expects all other authorities and parties to do the same. I make it clear that it will be for me to decide as I think right, within my terms of reference, the matters which will be the subject of my investigation.' The inquiry opened on 1 August 2003 and started taking evidence on 11 August 2003.

There had been calls for the inquiry to look into the question of the govern-ment's handling of intelligence information on Iraq, and many people felt it was regrettable that the scope of the inquiry was limited to the immediate pressures which might have prompted the weapons expert to take his life. But as the inquiry progressed, the wide range of witnesses who were called and the daily accounts and analysis of the hearing *in the press made it increasingly clear that Lord Hutton's findings and conclusions might well be of wide-ranging significance. This book provides an abridged edition of Lord Hutton's final report.*

# CONTENTS

List of persons  xi

Glossary  xvii

Extracts from Lord Hutton's report on the circumstances surrounding the death of Dr David Kelly

Chapter 1  3
Chapter 2  18
Chapter 3  43
Chapter 4  94
Chapter 5  146
Chapter 6  148
Chapter 7  199

# LIST OF PERSONS

*Mr A*  Civil servant with the Ministry of Defence counter proliferation arms control department; testified anonymously via video link (Interviewed)

*Absalom, Ruth*  Neighbour of Dr Kelly (Interviewed)

*Allan, Dr Richard*  Forensic toxicologist (Interviewed)

*Anderson, Donald*  Labour MP; chairperson of the Foreign Affairs Select Committee of the House of Commons (Interviewed)

*Avery, Roger*  Administrator and scientist at Virginia Tech University, USA; friend of Dr Kelly (Interviewed)

*Baldwin, Thomas*  Journalist, *The Times* (Interviewed)

*Bartlett, David*  Ambulance technician, Oxford Ambulance (Interviewed)

*Beaumont, Peter*  Foreign affairs editor, *Observer* (Interviewed)

*Blair, Tony*  Labour prime minister since 1997 (Interviewed)

*Blitz, James*  Political editor, *Financial Times* (Interviewed)

*Bosch, Olivia*  Senior research fellow at the Royal Institute of International Affairs, former UNSCOM inspector (Interviewed)

*Bradley, Peter*  Labour MP for Wrekin

*Broucher, David*  Foreign Office's ambassador-ranking permanent representative to the Conference on Disarmament in Geneva (Interviewed)

*Caldecott, Andrew, QC*  Counsel for the BBC

*Campbell, Alastair*  Former *Daily Mail* political editor; began work with Tony Blair after he became Labour leader in 1994 and became the prime minister's chief press spokesperson after Labour's election victory in 1997; moved to role of director of communications and strategy in 2001; resigned 26 August 2003 (Interviewed twice)

*Chapman, Paul*  Member, search and rescue team (Interviewed)

*Clark, John, Wing Commander*  MOD expert on arms control; colleague and friend who accompanied Dr Kelly on his appearances before parliamentary committees (Interviewed twice)

*Coe, Graham*  Police officer, Thames Valley Police (Interviewed)

*Cragg, Tony*  Deputy chief of the Defence Intelligence, September 1999 to January 2003 (Interviewed)

*Davies, Gavyn*  Chairman of the board of governors of the British Broadcasting

Corporation (Interviewed twice)

*Dearlove, Richard* Chief of the Secret Intelligence Service (Interviewed)

*Dingemans, James, QC* Senior counsel to the Hutton Inquiry

*Dyke, Greg* BBC director general (Interviewed)

*Evans, Michael* Defence editor, *The Times* (Interviewed)

*Flint, Julie* Middle East expert and former *Observer* reporter; friend of Dr Kelly; on 31 August 2003 released an unpublished article Dr Kelly had intended for inclusion in a report she was compiling on Iraq

*Franklin, Andrew* Police constable with the police support team, Thames Valley Police (Interviewed)

*French, Sir Joseph, Air Marshall* Chief of Defence Intelligence, November 2000 to April 2003 (Interviewed)

*Gilligan, Andrew* BBC defence correspondent responsible for Radio 4's *Today* programme report claiming that the government had 'sexed up' the September dossier (Inteviewed twice)

*Gompertz, Jeremy, QC* Counsel for the Kelly family

*Green, Roy* Forensic biologist (Interviewed)

*Harrison, James* Deputy director for counter proliferation and arms control in the Ministry of Defence (Interviewed twice)

*Hatfield, Richard* Personnel director, Ministry of Defence (Interviewed twice)

*Hawton, Keith* Director of the Centre for Suicide Research, Oxford University; advised on the effects of the pressure being placed on Dr Kelly in his last days (Interviewed twice)

*Hewitt, Gavin* BBC *10 o'clock News* special correspondent in contact with Dr Kelly (Interviewed)

*Hill, David* Succeeded Alastair Campbell as prime minister's director of communication

*Holmes, Louise* Member, search and rescue team (Interviewed)

*Hoon, Geoff* Secretary of state for defence (Interviewed twice)

*Howard, Martin* Deputy chief of defence intelligence, Ministry of Defence (Interviewed twice)

*Hughes, Lee Terence* Senior civil servant in the Department for Constitutional Affairs; secretary to the Hutton Inquiry (Interviewed)

*Hunt, Dr Nicholas* Forensic pathologist accredited to the Home Office (Interviewed)

*Hunt, Vanessa* Paramedic (Interviewed)

*Hutton (of Bresagh), Brian, Baron* A law lord since 1997, the sixth most senior of the 12 judges in the UK's highest court, the House of Lords; charged with heading the judicial inquiry into the circumstances surrounding the death of Dr David Kelly

*Jones, Dr Brian* Head in the scientific and technical directorate of the Defence Intelligence Analysis Staff at the time of the publication of the September dossier (Interviewed)

*Kelly, David, Dr* Scientist and biological weapons specialist: consultant to the MOD

*Kelly, Janice* Dr Kelly's widow (Interviewed)

*Kelly, Rachel* Dr Kelly's daughter (Interviewed)

*Kelly, Tom* Official spokesperson of Tony Blair (Interviewed twice)

*Knox, Peter* Junior counsel to the Hutton Inquiry

*Lamb, Patrick* Deputy head of the Foreign and Commonwealth Office's counter-proliferation department (Interviewed twice)

*Leith, John Barnabus (Barney)* Secretary, National Spiritual Association of Baha'is in the United Kingdom (Interviewed)

*Lloyd Jones, David, QC* Counsel for the Ministry of Defence

*Macdonald, Stephen* Assistant director on the central budget, security and safety for the Ministry of Defence (Interviewed)

*Mackinlay, Andrew* Labour member for Thurrock; member of the Commons Foreign Affairs Select Committee who questioned Dr Kelly (Interviewed)

*Mangold, Tom* Journalist, friend of Dr Kelly (Interviewed)

*Manning, Sir David* Former adviser to the prime minister on foreign policy and head of the overseas and defence secretariat in the Cabinet Office (Interviewed)

*Miller, Julian* Chief of the Cabinet Office's assessment staff, a body responsible to the Joint Intelligence Committee (Interviewed)

*Moonie, Lewis* Armed forces minister during the war in Iraq

*Norton-Taylor, Richard* Security affairs editor, *Guardian*

*Omand, Sir David* Security and intelligence coordinator in the Cabinet Office (Interviewed)

*Page, Michael* Assistant chief constable, Thames Valley Police (Interviewed)

*Pape, Sarah* Dr Kelly's sister (Interviewed)

*Pederson, Mai* US military linguist; introduced Dr Kelly to the Baha'i faith

*Potter, Leigh* Neighbour of Dr Kelly (Interviewed)

*Powell, Jonathan* Chief of staff at Downing Street (Interviewed)

*Rogers, Heather, QC* Counsel for Andrew Gilligan

*Rufford, Nick* *Sunday Times* reporter who interviewed Dr Kelly on 9 July 2003, the day after the MOD announced an official had come forward to say he could be Andrew Gilligan's source (Interviewed twice)

*Sambrook, Richard* BBC's director of news (Interviewed twice)

*Sammes, Anthony* Director of the Centre for Forensic Computing at Cranfield University (Interviewed)

*Sawyer, Jonathan Martyn* Police constable with the police support team, Thames Valley Police (Interviewed)

*Scarlett, John* Chairman of the Joint Intelligence Committee and head of the intelligence and securities secretariat in the Cabinet Office; former head of the Secret Intelligence Service (Interviewed twice)

*Scott, Dr Richard* Science Director at the Defence Science and Technology Laboratory (Interviewed)

*Shuttleworth, Dr* Dr Kelly's resource manager at the Defence Science and Technology Laboratory (Interviewed)

*Smith, Godric* Official spokesperson of Tony Blair (Interviewed twice)

*Sumption, Jonathan, QC* Counsel for the government

*Taylor, Ann* Labour MP for Dewsbury; chairperson of the Intelligence and Security Committee (Interviewed)

*Taylor, Richard* Special adviser to the secretary of state for defence (Interviewed)

*Taylor, Terence* Former UN weapons inspector, now president and executive director of the Institute of Strategic Studies, Washington, DC; friend of Dr Kelly who gave evidence to the Hutton Inquiry by satellite link from Australia (Interviewed)

*Teare, Pamela* Director of news, Ministry of Defence (Interviewed twice)

*Tebbit, Sir Kevin* Permanent undersecretary of state at the Ministry of Defence (Interviewed twice)

*Warner, Dr Malcolm* Dr Kelly's doctor (Interviewed)

*Watts, Susan* BBC *Newsnight* science editor who spoke to Dr Kelly about the September dossier (Interviewed)

*Webb, Geoffrey* Detective sergeant, Thames Valley Police (Interviewed)

*Wells, Dr Bryan* Director for counter proliferation and arms control at the Ministry of Defence and UK commissioner to UNMOVIC; Dr Kelly's line manager (Interviewed twice)

*Wilding, Edward* Computer investigator (Interviewed)

*Wilkins, David* Rachel Kelly's fiancé (Interviewed)

*Williams, John* Press secretary at the Foreign and Commonwealth Office (Interviewed)

*Wilson, Katherine* Chief press officer, Ministry of Defence (Interviewed)

# GLOSSARY

*Al-Qa'qa* Location in Iraq of a plant producing phosgene (which can be used as a chemical agent or as the precursor of a nerve agent)

*AMK* Andrew MacKinlay MP

*ANG* Andrew Gilligan

*BAH* Baha'i faith

*BBC* British Broadcasting Corporation

*BW* Biological warfare/weapons

*CAB* Cabinet Office

*COM* Files retrieved from Dr Kelly's home computer

*DIAS* Defence Intelligence Analysis Staff; part of the DIS

*DIS* Defence Intelligence Staff (of the Ministry of Defence)

*DOS* Published dossier

*DSTL* Defence Science and Technology Laboratory (Porton Down), an agency of the MOD

*FAC* Foreign Affairs Select Committee of the House of Commons; reports to Parliament

*FAM* Dr Kelly's family

*FIN* *Financial Times*

*GCHQ* Government Communications Headquarters; a Civil Service department under the ministerial responsibility of the secretary of state for foreign and commonwealth affairs

*GUA* *Guardian*

*ISC* Intelligence and Security Committee of the House of Commons, made up of nine senior politicians; oversees work of MI5, MI6, GCHQ; reports to the prime minister

*JIC* Joint Intelligence Committee; a Cabinet Office committee bringing together the chiefs of the intelligence and security services and senior policy makers in Whitehall, particularly from the Foreign Office and the Ministry of Defence; the body responsible for drawing up the September dossier

*JLF* Julie Flint

*MED* Media

*MOD* Ministry of Defence

*PAR* Parliament

*PEB* Peter Bradley MP

*PSY* Professor Hawton, Psychiatrist

*September dossier* Name given to the document 'Iraq's Weapons of Mass Destruction – The assessment of the British Government', published by the government on 24 September 2002, detailing 'the threat posed by Saddam Hussein's regime'

*SIS* Secret Intelligence Service (MI6)

*SJW* Susan Watts

*TIM* *The Times*

*TVP* Thames Valley Police

*UNMOVIC* United Nations Monitoring, Verification and Inspection Commission

*WMD* Weapons of mass destruction

# THE HUTTON INQUIRY

# CHAPTER I

On 18 July 2003 I was requested by the Rt Hon Lord Falconer of Thoroton, the Secretary of State for Constitutional Affairs, to conduct an Inquiry into the death of Dr David Kelly.

My terms of reference were 'urgently to conduct an investigation into the circumstances surrounding the death of Dr Kelly'. In my opinion these terms of reference required me to consider the circumstances preceding and leading up to the death of Dr Kelly insofar as (1) they might have had an effect on his state of mind and influenced his actions preceding and leading up to his death or (2) they might have influenced the actions of others which affected Dr Kelly preceding and leading up to his death. There has been a great deal of controversy and debate whether the intelligence in relation to weapons of mass destruction set out in the dossier published by the Government on 24 September 2002 was of sufficient strength and reliability to justify the Government in deciding that Iraq under Saddam Hussein posed such a threat to the safety and interests of the United Kingdom that military action should be taken against that country. This controversy and debate has continued because of the failure, up to the time of writing this report, to find weapons of mass destruction in Iraq. I gave careful consideration to the view expressed by a number of public figures and commentators that my terms of reference required or, at least, entitled me to consider this issue. However I concluded that a question of such wide import, which would involve the consideration of a wide range of evidence, is not one which falls within my terms of reference. The major controversy which arose following Mr Andrew Gilligan's broadcasts on the BBC Today programme on 29 May 2003 and which closely involved Dr Kelly arose from the allegations in the broadcasts (1) that the Government probably knew, before it decided to put it in its dossier of 24 September 2002, that the statement was wrong that the Iraqi military were able to deploy weapons of mass destruction within 45 minutes of a decision to do so and (2) that 10 Downing Street ordered the dossier to be sexed up. It was these allegations attacking the integrity of the Government which drew Dr Kelly into the controversy about the broadcasts and which I consider I should examine under my terms of reference. The issue whether, if approved by the Joint Intelligence Committee and believed by the Government to be reliable, the intelligence contained in the dossier was nevertheless unreliable is a separate issue which I consider does not fall within my terms of reference. There has also been debate as to the definition of the term 'weapons of mass destruction' (WMD) and as to the distinction between battlefield WMD and strategic WMD. Mr Gilligan's broadcasts on 29 May related to the claim in the dossier that chemical and biological weapons were deployable within 45 minutes and did not refer to the distinction between battlefield weapons, such as artillery and rockets, and strategic weapons, such as long range missiles, and a consideration of this issue does not fall within my terms of reference relating to the circumstances surrounding the death of Dr Kelly.

I further consider that one of my primary duties in carrying out my terms of reference is, after hearing the evidence of many witnesses, to state in considerable detail the relevant facts surrounding Dr Kelly's death and also, insofar as I can determine them, the motives and reasons operating in the minds of those who took various decisions and carried out various actions which affected Dr Kelly.

In order to enable the public to be as fully informed as possible I have also decided, rather than set out a summary of the evidence, to set out in this report many parts of the transcript of the evidence so that the public can read what the witnesses said and can understand why I have come to the conclusions which I state.

Whilst I stated at the preliminary sitting on 1 August that I did not sit to decide between conflicting cases advanced by interested parties who had opposing arguments to present, it has been inevitable in the course of the Inquiry that attention has focussed on the decisions and conduct of individual persons, and therefore I think it is right that I should express my opinion on the propriety or reasonableness of some of those decisions and actions.

I propose to commence by stating the facts which I consider have been established by the evidence which I have heard and by the documents put in evidence and many of these facts have not been in any real dispute. After stating the facts, I propose to turn to consider the issues which arise from those facts and to express my opinion in relation to them.

At the outset I state, for reasons which I will set out in greater detail in a later part of this report, that I am satisfied that Dr Kelly took his own life by cutting his left wrist and that his death was hastened by his taking Coproxamol tablets. I am further satisfied that there was no involvement by a third person in Dr Kelly's death.

I also consider it to be important to state in this early part of the report that I am satisfied that none of the persons whose decisions and actions I later describe ever contemplated that Dr Kelly might take his own life. I am further satisfied that none of those persons was at fault in not contemplating that Dr Kelly might take his own life. Whatever pressures and strains Dr Kelly was subjected to by the decisions and actions taken in the weeks before his death, I am satisfied that no one realised or should have realised that those pressures and strains might drive him to take his own life or contribute to his decision to do so.

The facts which I consider have been established by the evidence given in the course of the Inquiry are the following and I shall return to discuss some of these facts in greater detail in later parts of this report.

Dr Kelly was a biologist by training, who held degrees from a number of universities and he was a very highly qualified specialist in the field of biology. In 1984 he joined the Ministry of Defence (MoD) and was appointed to head the microbiology division at the chemical and biological defence establishment at Porton Down in Wiltshire. The nature of Dr Kelly's employment within the Civil Service later became somewhat complex. In April 1995 the Defence Evaluation and Research Agency (DERA) was established as an agency of the MoD and Dr Kelly's personnel management and employment formally passed from the MoD to DERA. In 1996 Dr Kelly was appointed on secondment to the Proliferation and Arms Control Secretariat (PACS) within the MoD and he worked as an adviser to PACS and to the Non-Proliferation Department of the Foreign and Commonwealth Office (FCO) on Iraq's chemical and biological weapons capabilities and on the work of the United Nations Monitoring, Verification and Inspection Commission (UNMOVIC). Dr Kelly was also responsible for providing advice to the Defence Intelligence Staff (DIS) of the MoD and to the Secret Intelligence Service (SIS) on Iraq. Dr Kelly's secondment was principally funded by the FCO for whom Dr Kelly carried out a substantial proportion of his work. From 1991 to 1998 Dr Kelly made 37 visits to Iraq in the course of his duties and took very few holidays. In 2001 the part of DERA which employed Dr Kelly became part of Defence Science and Technology Laboratory (DSTL) which is a Trading Fund of the MoD and DSTL became Dr Kelly's employer during the remainder of his secondment to the MoD which continued until his death.

In the mid 1990s Dr Kelly became dissatisfied with his salary and grading after DERA had created a new salary and grading structure and moved away from the general Civil Service structure. It appears that Dr Kelly had not been properly assimilated within the DERA salary scales and it appears that this may have happened because he was working abroad so much. Dr Kelly sought assistance on a number of occasions from the officials who were then his line managers. They intervened on his behalf and Dr Kelly was eventually regraded and advanced to a higher grade in February 2002. One of his line managers, Dr Shuttleworth described Dr Kelly as being concerned and frustrated but not bitter about his salary and grading.

In the early 1990s Dr Kelly became involved in the analysis of information about the biological and warfare programme of the Soviet Union and he went to Russia as a member of the Anglo American team visiting biotechnology facilities in different parts of Russia and played a leading role in that inspection. His work in Russia was most successful and he was highly respected by both the British and American members of the team.

In 1991 Dr Kelly became one of the chief weapons inspectors in Iraq on behalf of the United Nations Special Commission (UNSCOM) and from 1991 onwards was deeply involved in investigating the biological warfare programme of the Iraqi regime. These investigations resulted in 1995 in UNSCOM making a breakthrough and forcing the Iraqi regime to admit that it did have a biological warfare programme. During the 1990s Dr Kelly built up a high reputation as a weapons inspector, not only in the United Kingdom but internationally, and he was described in evidence by the journalist and author, Mr Tom Mangold, who knew him well, as the 'inspector's inspector'. The contribution made by Dr Kelly and the importance of his work was recognised by the Government and in 1996 he was appointed Companion of the Order of St Michael and St George (C.M.G.), the material part of the citation for the award stating:

> ...he devised the scientific basis for the enhanced biological warfare defence programme and led strong research groups in many key areas. Following the Gulf War he led the first biological warfare inspection in Iraq and has spent most of his time since either in Iraq or at various sites in the former Soviet Union helping to shed light on past biological warfare related activities and assisting the UK/US RUS trilateral confidence building process. He has pursued this work tirelessly and with good humour despite the significant hardship, hostility and personal risk encountered during extended periods of service in both countries. In 1991 he was appointed adviser to the UN Special Commission (UNSCOM). His efforts in his specialist field have had consequences of international significance.

It appears that in May 2003 Dr Kelly was being considered for a further award (which might well have been a knighthood as he had already been awarded the C.M.G.) because a minute to Heads of Department in the FCO dated 9 May 2003 requested recommendations for the Diplomatic Service List and on 14 May an official wrote the following manuscript note on the minute:

> How about David Kelly? (Iraq being topical).

•••

On 24 September 2002 the Government published a dossier entitled:
IRAQ'S WEAPONS OF MASS DESTRUCTION
THE ASSESSMENT OF THE BRITISH GOVERNMENT

This dossier contained a foreword by the Prime Minister:

The document published today is based, in large part, on the work of the Joint Intelligence Committee (JIC). The JIC is at the heart of the British intelligence machinery. It is chaired by the Cabinet Office and made up of the heads of the UK's three Intelligence and Security Agencies, the Chief of Defence Intelligence, and senior officials from key government departments. For over 60 years the JIC has provided regular assessments to successive Prime Ministers and senior colleagues on a wide range of foreign policy and international security issues.

Its work, like the material it analyses, is largely secret. It is unprecedented for the Government to publish this kind of document. But in light of the debate about Iraq and Weapons of Mass Destruction (WMD), I wanted to share with the British public the reasons why I believe this issue to be a current and serious threat to the UK national interest.

In recent months, I have been increasingly alarmed by the evidence from inside Iraq that despite sanctions, despite the damage done to his capability in the past, despite the UN Security Council's Resolutions expressly outlawing it, and despite his denials, Saddam Hussein is continuing to develop WMD, and with them the ability to inflict real damage upon the region, and the stability of the world.

Gathering intelligence inside Iraq is not easy. Saddam's is one of the most secretive and dictatorial regimes in the world. So I believe people will understand why the Agencies cannot be specific about the sources, which have formed the judgments in this document, and why we cannot publish everything we know. We cannot, of course, publish the detailed raw intelligence. I and other Ministers have been briefed in detail on the intelligence and are satisfied as to its authority. I also want to pay tribute to our Intelligence and Security Services for the often extraordinary work that they do.

What I believe the assessed intelligence has established beyond doubt is that Saddam has continued to produce chemical and biological weapons, that he continues in his efforts to develop nuclear weapons, and that he has been able to extend the range of his ballistic missile programme. I also believe that, as stated in the document, Saddam will now do his utmost to try to conceal his weapons from UN inspectors.

The picture presented to me by the JIC in recent months has become more not less worrying. It is clear that, despite sanctions, the policy of containment has not worked sufficiently well to prevent Saddam from developing these weapons.

I am in no doubt that the threat is serious and current, that he has made progress on WMD, and that he has to be stopped.

Saddam has used chemical weapons, not only against an enemy state, but against his own people. Intelligence reports make clear that he sees the building up of his WMD capability, and the belief overseas that he would use these weapons, as vital to his strategic interests, and in particular his goal of regional domination. And the document discloses that his military planning allows for some of the WMD to be ready within 45 minutes of an order to use them.

I am quite clear that Saddam will go to extreme lengths, indeed has already done so, to hide these weapons and avoid giving them up.

In today's inter-dependent world, a major regional conflict does not stay confined to the region in question. Faced with someone who has shown himself capable of using WMD, I believe the international community has to stand up for itself and ensure its authority is upheld.

The threat posed to international peace and security, when WMD are in the hands of a brutal and aggressive regime like Saddam's, is real. Unless we face up to the threat, not only do we risk undermining the authority of the UN, whose resolutions he defies, but more importantly and in the longer term, we place at risk the lives and prosperity of our own people.

The case I make is that the UN Resolutions demanding he stops his WMD programme are being flouted; that since the inspectors left four years ago he has continued with this programme; that the inspectors must be allowed back in to do their job properly; and that if he refuses, or if he makes it impossible for them to do their job, as he has done in the past, the international community will have to act.

I believe that faced with the information available to me, the UK Government has been right to support the demands that this issue be confronted and dealt with. We must ensure that he does not get to use the weapons he has, or get hold of the weapons he wants.

The Executive Summary stated:

As well as the public evidence, however, significant additional information is available to the Government from secret intelligence sources, described in more detail in this paper. This intelligence cannot tell us about everything. However, it provides a fuller picture of Iraqi plans and capabilities. It shows that Saddam Hussein attaches great importance to possessing weapons of mass destruction which he regards as the basis for Iraq's regional power. It shows that he does not regard them only as weapons of last resort. He is ready to use them, including against his own population, and is determined to retain them, in breach of United Nations Security Council Resolutions (UNSCR).

Intelligence also shows that Iraq is preparing plans to conceal evidence of these weapons, including incriminating documents, from renewed inspections. And it confirms that despite sanctions and the policy of containment, Saddam has continued to make progress with his illicit weapons programmes.

As a result of the intelligence we judge that Iraq has:

... military plans for the use of chemical and biological weapons, including against its own Shia population. Some of these weapons are deployable within 45 minutes of an order to use them.

Chapter 3 headed: 'THE CURRENT POSITION: 1998–2002' stated:

1. This chapter sets out what we know of Saddam Hussein's chemical, biological, nuclear and ballistic missile programmes, drawing on all the available evidence. While it takes account of the results from UN inspections and other publicly available information, it also draws heav-

ily on the latest intelligence about Iraqi efforts to develop their programmes and capabilities since 1998. The main conclusions are that:

... Iraq's military forces are able to use chemical and biological weapons, with command, control and logistical arrangements in place. The Iraqi military are able to deploy these weapons within forty five minutes of a decision to do so.

...

Subsequently, intelligence has become available from reliable sources which complements and adds to previous intelligence and confirms the JIC assessment that Iraq has chemical and biological weapons. The intelligence also shows that the Iraqi leadership has been discussing a number of issues related to these weapons. This intelligence covers:

Saddam's willingness to use chemical and biological weapons: Intelligence indicates that as part of Iraq's military planning, Saddam is willing to use chemical and biological weapons, including against his own Shia population. Intelligence indicates that the Iraqi military are able to deploy chemical or biological weapons within forty five minutes of an order to do so.

The rules governing the disclosure of information by civil servants

The rules governing the disclosure of information by civil servants in the MoD are set out as follows in Volume 7 of the MoD Personnel Manual:

Section 6: Disclosure of Information
6.1 Principles governing disclosure of information

This section describes the principles governing the public disclosure of information by serving or former members of the Department and sets out the rules that apply those principles to specific cases. The activities governed by this section are:

public lectures and speeches, interviews with or communications to the press or other media, film, radio and television appearances and statements to non-Governmental bodies, including MOD-sponsored conferences and seminars; ...

You must not make comment on, or make disclosure of:

classified or 'in confidence' information;

relations between civil servants and Ministers, and advice given to Ministers;

politically controversial issues; ...

information that would conflict with MOD interests ...anything that the MOD would regard as objectionable about individuals or organisations;

Paragraph 10 of Annex A to the Civil Service Code states:

Civil servants should not without authority disclose official information which has been communicated in confidence within the Administration, or received in confidence from others. Nothing in the Code should be taken as overriding existing statutory or common law obligations to keep confidential, or to disclose, certain information. They should not seek to frustrate or influence the policies, decisions or actions of Ministers, Assembly Secretaries or the National Assembly as a body by the unauthorised, improper or premature disclosure outside the Administration of any information to which they have had access as civil servants.

The DSTL procedure for conduct rules (which say on the title page that DSTL is part of the MoD) state:

8.4 Media activities

12

8.4.1 It is important to dispel any impression, however unfounded, that there is a conflict of interest between a particular activity and the responsibilities of an employee. There is no exhaustive list of activities that fall into this category, but it is in everyone (sic) interest for individuals to seek approval before indulging in any such activity and to ensure that records are kept.

8.4.2 Examples of activities that may conflict with the responsibilities of employees are:

press announcements (these should be referred to Head of Corporate Affairs);

broadcasts and media interviews and public speaking (these should be referred to Head of Corporate Affairs);

lecturing or speaking at conferences and seminars, especially on matters of political sensitivity. The procedure for public disclosure of Dstl official information is to be followed. Employees should not attend political conferences in their official capacity without prior permission from their Department Manager;

completing external questionnaires (e.g. those asking for detailed information about the organisation). Any doubts should be referred to Head of Corporate Affairs;

publishing books, writing papers for publication. Applications to publish are to be made on a completed Dstl application for permission to publish (Form 199 – reference 10).

One of Dr Kelly's roles in the course of his work was to speak to the media and institutions on Iraq issues and parts of his Performance and Development Assessment for the year April 2002 to March 2003 dated 12 April 2003 are as follows:

Statement of your roles and responsibilities:

Adviser to Proliferation Arms Control Secretariat, MOD and Non-proliferation Department, FCO on Iraq's chemical and biological weapons capabilities, UNMOVIC activities, and CWC/BWC issues. Adviser to DIS and SIS on Iraq.

Adviser to UNMOVIC on chemical biological weapons and inspector training.

Communicating Iraq issues to the media and Institutions

•••

**Objective**: Communication of Iraq issues externally  (Date & initial)

**Your comments**: To continue making contributions to the deliberations of International Institutions and providing informed contributions to the international media and press.

**Managers' comments:** David has lectured widely on Iraqi WMD issues, is much sought for attendance at international conferences and as appropriate has provided media briefings

Annexed to Dr Kelly's Performance and Development Assessment for April 2002 to March 2003 was the following list of attendance at conferences and contacts with the media:

11th & 12th November 2002

Organization for the Prohibition of Chemical Weapons, The Hague, The Netherlands 'Protection Network'

18th to 20th November 2002

International Institute for Strategic Studies, London: Conference 'Iraq: Invasion or inspections' 31st January and 1st February 2003

Attributable and unattributable briefings plus interviews on Iraq, Russia, Weapons, Anthrax and Smallpox.

Television & Radio: Channel Four, Australian Broadcasting Company, Canadian Broadcasting Company, Tokyo Broadcasting Systems, CNN, CBS, ABC, Radio Netherlands, BBC four, BBC 24hours/World Service, BBC local radio (London, Wales).

News Media: Guardian, Daily Telegraph, The Times, New York Times, Washington Post, Los Angeles Times, Newsweek, Herald Tribune, and Wall Street Journal.

•••

On 10 October 2002 Sir Kevin Tebbit, the Permanent Under-Secretary of State at the MoD, sent a minute to senior officials in the MoD in relation to contacts with the media:

CONTACTS WITH THE MEDIA

For a number of reasons the MOD and the Armed Forces are likely to find themselves the subject of more than usual media interest over the next six months. We ought to be as open as we can in explaining what we are doing and why. Equally, there is some information which must remain confidential if the Department and the Armed Forces are properly to perform their functions. It would be timely to restate the basic principles.

2. First, there are clear rules about seeking approval for media interviews and other contacts which must be followed in all cases. These are set out in DCI 313/99. In particular, proposals for contact by 2 Star offi-

cers/officials and above must be approved by Ministers. It is the responsibility of the officers/officials concerned to ensure that DGCC and his staff and/or the Corporate Communications and Media Ops staff embedded in TLB areas are informed of proposed media contacts so that appropriate guidance and advice can be provided. Unless there are very good reasons otherwise, communications staff should be present during interviews.

3. Second, submissions to Ministers and others must include a section on presentation covering both external and internal audiences, that is drawn up in conjunction with DGCC staffs. In particular, it must be explicitly acknowledged in the advice that goes forward that D News (or DGCC himself) has been consulted and is content.

4. Finally, a reminder of what CDS and I stated on 12 June about unauthorised leaks to the media. These are counterproductive and damaging to the reputation of the MOD in the eyes of the public and other Government Departments. They are also unprofessional and corrosive of trust and morale. In addition to being disciplinary offences, they could also lead to prosecution after criminal investigation.

5. I look to DMB members, TLB Holders and all senior line managers to enforce these guidelines.

•••

The Intelligence and Security Committee (ISC), a Committee of Members of Parliament, in its Report of September 2003 described its functions as follows:

i. The Intelligence and Security Committee (ISC) is established under the Intelligence Services Act 1994 to examine the expenditure, administration and policy of the United Kingdom's three intelligence and security Agencies: the Security Service, the Secret Intelligence Service (SIS) and the Government Communications Headquarters (GCHQ). The

16

Committee also takes evidence from the Security and Intelligence Co-ordinator, the Chairman of the Joint Intelligence Committee (JIC) and the Defence Intelligence Staff (DIS), as well as departments and other organisations that receive secret intelligence from the Agencies.

ii. The Prime Minister, in consultation with the leaders of the two main opposition parties, appoints the ISC members. Nominations for the membership of the Committee are put forward by the Government and Opposition whips, in a broadly similar way to the nomination of select committee members.

iii. The Committee reports directly to the Prime Minister and through him to Parliament by the publication of the Committee's Reports. The members are notified under the Official Secrets Act 1989 and, as such, operate within 'the ring of secrecy'. The Committee sees significant amounts of classified material in carrying out its duties and it takes evidence from Cabinet Ministers and senior officials – all of which is used to formulate its Reports.

iv. When laying a Report before Parliament, the Prime Minister, in consultation with the Committee, excludes any parts of the Report (indicated by the *** in the text) that would be prejudicial to the continuing discharge of the functions of the three intelligence and security Agencies. To date, no material has been excluded without the Committee's consent.

It appears from that Report that the ISC decided about the start of May 2003 to examine the intelligence relating to Iraq's Weapons of Mass Destruction (WMD) and paragraph 12 of its Report states:

On 8 May 2003, the Committee Chairman, the Rt. Hon. Ann Taylor, MP, wrote to the Chairman of the JIC to request all the JIC Assessments relating to Iraq and its WMD dating back to August 1990 and supporting intelligence.

# CHAPTER 2

On 7 May 2003 Ms Susan Watts, the Science Editor of BBC Newsnight telephoned Dr Kelly and had a discussion with him about a number of matters relating to Iraq. Ms Watts' brief shorthand notes made in the course of the discussion record that Dr Kelly said to her in respect of the statement in the Government's dossier that chemical and biological weapons were deployable within 45 minutes of an order to use them:

> mistake to put in ... A Campbell seeing something in there ... NB single source ... but not corroborated ... sounded good

On 22 May 2003, by prior arrangement, Dr Kelly met Mr Andrew Gilligan, the defence and diplomatic correspondent of the Today programme on BBC Radio 4, in the Charing Cross Hotel, London, and had a discussion with him. I will return to this discussion in more detail in a later part of this report.

On the evening of 28 May Mr Gilligan telephoned Mrs Kate Wilson the chief press officer at the MoD and spoke to her about the Today programme to be broadcast the next morning. I will return to this telephone conversation in more detail in a later part of this report.

On 29 May 2003 in the Today programme on BBC Radio 4 Mr Gilligan broadcast a number of reports relating to the dossier published by the Government on 24 September 2002. These reports were preceded at 6.00am by the following headlines read by Mr John Humphreys and Ms Corrie Corfield:

JH: Tony Blair is going to Iraq today. There have been new accusations over the reasons for fighting the war...

CC: Tony Blair will set foot on Iraqi soil today – just seven weeks after Saddam

Hussein was swept from power. His visit comes amid continuing controversy about the likelihood of weapons of mass destruction being found. The US Defence Secretary, Donald Rumsfeld, has suggested that the weapons might have been destroyed before the fighting began. This report is from our political correspondent, John Pienaar ('JP'), who's travelling with the Prime Minister.

JP: This morning, Tony Blair becomes the first Western leader to land in Iraq since the war, a symbolic appearance and one that will test his political skills as well as his flair for presentation. The visit is about thanking the troops and weighing up the task of reconstruction, according to Mr Blair, not triumphalism. Even so, he and his team will want to cultivate the images that will tell the tale of a liberated people. The problems and bitterness of the aftermath of war will be discussed behind the scenes in talks with British officials, Iraq civilians and the military. Today's visit will be brief. The business of rebuilding Iraq, politically and economically, and the search for the elusive weapons of mass destruction, looks like continuing perhaps for rather longer than Mr Blair might have hoped.

CC: A senior official involved in preparing the Government's dossier on Iraqi weapons of mass destruction has told this programme that the document was rewritten just before publication – to make it more exciting. An assertion that some of the weapons could be activated within 45 minutes was among the claims added at a late stage. The official claimed that the intelligence services were unhappy with the changes, which he said were ordered by Downing Street.

At 6.07am the following was broadcast:

JH: The government is facing more questions this morning over its claims about weapons of mass destruction in Iraq. Our defence correspondent is Andrew Gilligan. This in particular Andy is Tony Blair saying, they'd be ready to go within forty five minutes.

Andrew Gilligan (AG): That's right, that was the central claim in his dossier which he published in September, the main erm, case if you like against er, against Iraq and the main statement of the British government's belief of what it thought Iraq was up to and what we've been told by one of the senior officials in charge of drawing up that dossier was that, actually the government probably erm, knew that that forty five minute figure was wrong, even before it decided to put it in. What this person says, is that a week before the publication date of the dossier, it was actually rather erm, a bland production. It didn't, the, the draft prepared for Mr Blair by the Intelligence Agencies actually didn't say very much more than was public knowledge already and erm, Downing Street, our source says ordered a week before publication, ordered it to be sexed up, to be made more exciting and ordered more facts to be er, to be discovered.

JH: When you say 'more facts to be discovered', does that suggest that they may not have been facts?

AG: Well, erm, our source says that the dossier, as it was finally published, made the Intelligence Services unhappy, erm, because, to quote erm the source he said, there was basically, that there was, there was, there was unhappiness because it didn't reflect, the considered view they were putting forward, that's a quote from our source and essentially, erm, the forty five minute point er, was, was probably the most important thing that was added. Erm, and the reason it hadn't been in the original draft was that it was, it was only erm, it only came from one source and most of the other claims were from two, and the intelligence agencies say they don't really believe it was necessarily true because they thought the person making the claim had actually made a mistake, it got, had got mixed up.

JH: Does any of this matter now, all this, all these months later? The war's been fought and won.

AG: Well the forty five minutes isn't just a detail, it did go to the heart of the government's case that Saddam was an imminent threat and it was repeated four times in the dossier, including by the Prime Minister himself, in the foreword; so I think it probably does matter. Clearly, you know, if erm, if it, if it was, if it was wrong, things do, things are, got wrong in good faith but if they knew it was wrong before they actually made the claim, that's perhaps a bit more serious.

JH: Andrew, many thanks; more about that later.

At 7.32am the following was broadcast:

JH: Twenty eight minutes to eight. Tony Blair had quite a job persuading the country and indeed his own MPs to support the invasion of Iraq; his main argument was that Saddam had weapons of mass destruction that threatened us all. None of those weapons has been found. Now our defence correspondent, Andrew Gilligan, has found evidence that the government's dossier on Iraq that was produced last September, was cobbled together at the last minute with some unconfirmed material that had not been approved by the Security Services. Now you told us about this earlier on the programme Andy, and we've had a statement from 10 Downing Street that says it's not true, and let me just quote what they said to you. 'Not one word of the dossier was not entirely the work of the intelligence agencies'. Sorry to submit you to this sort of English but there we are. I think we know what they mean. Are you suggesting, let's be very clear about this, that it was not the work of the intelligence agencies.

AG: No, the information which I'm told was dubious did come from the agencies, but they were unhappy about it, because they didn't think it should have been in there. They thought it was, it was not corroborated sufficiently, and they actually thought it was wrong, they thought the informant concerned erm, had got it wrong, they thought he'd misunderstood what was happening.

I mean let's, let's go through this. This is the dossier that was published in September last year, erm, probably the most substantial statement of the government's case against Iraq. You'll remember that the Commons was recalled to debate it, Tony Blair made the opening speech. It is not the same as the famous dodgy dossier, the one that was copied off the internet, that came later. This is quite a serious document. It dominated the news that day and you open up the dossier and the first thing you see is a preface written by Tony Blair that includes the following words, 'Saddam's military planning allows for some weapons of mass destruction to be ready within forty five minutes of an order to deploy them'. Now that claim has come back to haunt Mr Blair because if the weapons had been that readily to hand, they probably would have been found by now. But you know, it could have been an honest mistake, but what I have been told is that the government knew that claim was questionable, even before the war, even before they wrote it in their dossier.

I have spoken to a British official who was involved in the preparation of the dossier, and he told me that until the week before it was published, the draft dossier produced by the Intelligence Services, added little to what was already publicly known. He said: 'It was transformed in the week before it was published, to make it sexier. The classic example was the statement that weapons of mass destruction were ready for use within forty five minutes. That information was not in the original draft. It was included in the dossier against our wishes, because it wasn't reliable. Most things in the dossier were double source, but, that was single source, and we believed that the source was wrong.

Now this official told us that the transformation of the dossier took place at the behest of Downing Street, and he added: 'Most people in intelligence weren't happy with the dossier, because it didn't reflect the considered view they were putting forward'. Now I want to stress that this official and others I've spoken to, do still believe that Iraq did have some sort of weapons of mass destruction programme. 'I believe it is about 30% likely there was a chemical weapons programme in the six months before the war and considerably more likely, that there was a biological weapons programme. We think Hans Blix down-played a couple of potentially interesting pieces of evidence, but the weapons programmes were small: sanctions did limit the programmes'.

The official also added quite an interesting note about what has happened as a result since the war, of the capture of some Iraqi WMD scientists: 'We don't have a great deal more information yet than we had before. We have not got very much out of the detainees yet.'

Now the forty five minutes really is, is not just a detail, it did go to the heart of the government's case that Saddam was an imminent threat, and it was repeated a further three times in the body of the dossier, and I understand that the parliamentary intelligence and security committee is going to conduct an enquiry in to the claims made by the British Government about Iraq, and it is obviously exactly this kind of issue that will be at the heart of their investigation.

JH: Andrew Gilligan, many thanks.

Later in the Today programme Mr Adam Ingram MP, the Armed Forces Minister, was interviewed by Mr John Humphreys and in the course of the interview Mr Humphreys put to him the following allegation:

Can I tell you what the allegation was because I think you may have been a little misled on that. The allegation was not that it was concocted by Number 10, the allegation was that a report was produced. It went to Number 10. It was then sent back to be sexed up a little, I'm using not my own words, but the words of our source, as you know. Now, given that, is it possible that ...

AI: Well it's not true that, that allegation.

JH: That isn't true.

AI: No, it's not true. And you know Number 10 has denied that.

Also on 29 May on BBC Radio 5 Live Breakfast programme at 7.50am Mr Gilligan broadcast a report relating to the September dossier in which he said:

Presenter (P): Good Morning.

A senior official involved in preparing the Government's dossier on Iraqi weapons of mass destruction has said the document was rewritten just before it was published to apparently „make it more exciting". The official said the intelligence services were unhappy with the changes. Let's talk to Andrew Gilligan our defence correspondent.

Hello Andrew.

Andrew Gilligan: Hello

P: This was the dossier published what, last September by the Government?

Andrew: That's right. This is not the famous 'dodgy dossier' that was copied off the internet, that came later. This was a much more substantial effort. Parliament was recalled to discuss it. Tony Blair made the opening speech in Parliament, em and, and it dominated the news that day. It was, it's the most substantial statement of the Government's case against Iraq.

P: And what, according to the intelligence services were the problems with it?

Andrew: Well, the draft they originally produced they tell me was actually not terribly exciting, it didn't add very much to what we already knew publicly. What any, kind of anyone who'd followed the story would know publicly, and it didn't satisfy Downing Street and they said eh, look, you know, is there anything more this – can, can we make this a bit more exciting please.

Em, and er, they mentioned a few things which they weren't very happy with and at Downing Street's insistence those were written into the document and one of the main things that em, that they weren't very happy with was this claim that Iraq could deploy its biological and chemical weapons within 45 minutes.

Now we now (sic), we can be pretty sure now that that claim was actually wrong. Because if they could deploy within that short a time we'd have found the weapons by now, you know if they were that handy then they would have been more or less lying around er, and easily, easy for the troops to find in six weeks. Em, now, you know, what I thought to be honest was that that eh, that claim was wrong in good faith. Em, but er, what my intelligence service source says is that em essentially they were always suspicious about this claim, they did not want it to appear in the document, they did not put it in their original draft because em most of the assertions in the dossier were double sourced, this was only one source, and they didn't believe the source, they thought he had got mixed up. They thought he had got mixed up between the time it took to assemble a conventional er missile assembly and em aa and the idea that em Saddam had a er weapons of mass destruction missile assembly.

P: So, I mean the implications that the, that Downing Street asked for it to be hyped up to help convince the doubters.

Andrew: Yeah, and, and they're not very happy. I mean the actual quote from my source was 'most people in intelligence weren't happy with the dossier because it didn't reflect the considered view they were putting forward' and it was a matter of language and nuance as much as em er as actual detail. But the 45 minutes was very important because it went to the heart of the Government's case that Saddam was an imminent threat.

P: Absolutely. But, fundamentally, the intelligence services did believe, did have intelligence that Iraq did have weapons of mass destruction.

Andrew: Yeah, they, they do believe that Iraq had a programme and what my source said was that he believed it was about 30% likely that there was a chemical weapons programme even in the six months before the war, and more likely considerably more likely, that there was a biological weapons programme. But he said the programmes they thought were small and not necessarily an imminent threat and sanctions did limit the programmes and, and eh, you know that, that the the issue is about tone and, er and nuance, …[Presenter: hmmm] ... it really is as much as anything else and, and really had they said all that in, in the way they wanted to it wouldn't have been nearly as compelling a case.

P: And, and in a word, the intelligence services, do they still believe weapons of mass destruction will be found in Iraq at some point?

Andrew: They believe there were some. Em, their (sic) not sure what to believe now to be honest, because what they are saying is, em, you know, they were int ..., they have been interrogating all these em, all these people that they have captured and, and they are not telling them very much.

P: Thank you very much Andrew.

On 29 May around 2pm London time Mr Gavin Hewitt, a special correspondent for BBC News, telephoned Dr Kelly who was in New York and had a telephone conversation with him in relation to matters in Iraq. In his evidence to the Inquiry Mr Hewitt described what Dr Kelly told him as follows:

> we got straight on to the question of his kind of overall view of the dossier and very early on in the conversation – and these are his precise words. He said:"No. 10 spin came into play". I asked him what he meant by this and he elaborated and he said he felt the essential quality of the intelligence provided by the Intelligence Services was fundamentally reasonable. That is the phrase, 'fundamental information reasonable'; but – and this is where his reservation came in – he felt that the dossier had been presented in a very black and white way. He expressed some caution about that. I think he would have liked more caveats. I think he would have been comfortable, from what he said, that it would have been more measured, in his view. He then went on to give me his views about weapons of mass destruction and he was clear, throughout this fairly brief conversation, he believed that weapons of mass destruction did exist in Iraq, but he did not feel that they constituted a major threat and he felt that even if they were found they would not be found

26

as a massive arsenal.

On 29 May on BBC Television 10pm News Mr Hewitt broadcast the following report in relation to the September dossier:

> This is really a story about trust. It begins here at MI6, the headquarters of the intelligence service. Some of those who work here are said to be uneasy about what the government did with information they passed on about Iraq. There were claims today that when Downing Street received the dossier it wanted it toughened up. When it was eventually published it did contain some dramatic warnings ...

> The government acknowledged today that the forty five minute threat was based on a single source, it wasn't corroborated. This has rattled some MPs who are calling for an investigation ...

> The government said today that every word within the dossier was the work of the security services. There had been no pressure from Number 10 ...

> But others with experience in the intelligence community say there were some murmurings about the final wording of a dossier ...

> I have spoken to one of those who was consulted on the dossier. Six months work was apparently involved. But in the final week before publication, some material was taken out, some material put in. His judgment, some spin from Number Ten did come into play. Even so the intelligence community remains convinced weapons of mass destruction will be found in Iraq. Only then will all the doubts go away.

The entirety of what was said in the 10pm news in relation to the September dossier is set out in appendix 2.

On 30 May 2003 Ms Susan Watts contacted Dr Kelly and had a lengthy telephone conversation with him which she recorded on a tape recorder and I am satisfied that she made an accurate transcript of that conversation. Part of that transcript is as follows:

SW: OK, um While I'm sure since you've been in New York I don't know whether you've been following the kind of the rumpus that's erupted over here over the ... spat between the intelligence service and the umm ...

DK: I guessed something was up – I read the Times this am and I could see there was something there and I think this follows on from what was happening in the states with Rumsfeld's comments.

SW: yes it's partly prompted by Rumsfeld – two statements by Rumsfeld – the first one saying that it was 'possible' the weapons were destroyed before the war started and then he went on I think in another speech yesterday to say that the use of the argument on the position on WMD was for bureaucratic reasons rather than being the prime motive for the war, which is a rather vague statement.

DK: yes

SW: But what intrigued me and which made, prompted me to ring you, (huh) was the quotes yesterday on the Today programme about the 45 minutes part of the dossier.

DK: yep. We spoke about this before of course ....

SW: We have

DK: I think you know my views on that.

SW: Yes, I've looked back at my notes and you were actually quite specific at that time – I may have missed a trick on that one, but err

(both laugh)

SW: you were more specific than the source on the Today programme – not that that necessarily means that it's not one and the same person … but, um in fact you actually referred to Alastair Campbell in that conversation ….

DK: err yep yep … with you? …

SW: yes

DK: I mean I did talk to Gavin Hewitt yesterday – he phoned me in New York, so he may have picked up on what I said … because I would have said exactly the same as I said to you ….

SW: Yes, so he presumably decided not to name Alastair Campbell himself but just to label this as Number 10 ….

DK: yep yep

SW: are you getting much flak over that?

DK: me? No, not yet anyway I was in New York … (laughs)

SW: yes good timing I suppose

DK: I mean they wouldn't think it was me, I don't think. Maybe they would, maybe they wouldn't. I don't know.

SW: um so is that the only item in the report that you had concerns over being single-sourced rather than double-sourced?

DK: You have to remember I'm not part of the intelligence community – I'm a user of intelligence … of course I'm very familiar with a lot of it, that's why I'm asked to comment on it … but I'm not deeply embedded into that …xxx

... So some of it I really can't comment because I don't know whether it's single-sourced or not

SW: but on the 45 minutes

DK: oh that I knew because I knew the concern about the statement ... it was a statement that was made and it just got out of all proportion ... you know someone ... They were desperate for information ... they were pushing hard for information which could be released .. that was one that popped up and it was seized on ... and it was unfortunate that it was ... which is why there is the argument between the intelligence services and cabinet office/number ten, because things were picked up on, and once they've picked up on it you can't pull it back, that's the problem ...

SW: but it was against your advice that they should publish it?

DK: I wouldn't go as strongly as to say ... that particular bit, because I was not involved in the assessment of it ... no ... I can't say that it was against MY advice ... I was uneasy with it ... I mean my problem was I could give other explanations ... which I've indicated to you ... that it was the time to erect something like a scud missile or it was the time to fill a 40 barrel, multi-barrel rocket launcher

.... (Next 5 words physically removed from tape ... not present on Monday 14/7/03 .... assume due to rubbing as tape constantly re-wound)

...("all sorts of reasons why") 45 minutes might well be important and ... I mean I have no idea who de-briefed this guy quite often it's someone who has no idea of the topic and the information comes through and people then use it as they see fit ....

SW: so it wasn't as if there were lots of people saying don't put it in don't put it in ... it's just it was in there and was seized upon ... rather than number ten specifically going against ...?

30

DK: there were lots of people saying that - I mean it was an interesting week before the dossier was put out because there were so many things in there that people were saying well … we're not so sure about that, or in fact they were happy with it being in but not expressed the way that it was, because you know the word-smithing is actually quite important and the intelligence community are a pretty cautious lot on the whole but once you get people putting it/presenting it for public consumption then of course they use different words. I don't think they're being wilfully dishonest I think they just think that that's the way the public will appreciate it best. I'm sure you have the same problem as a journalist don't you, sometimes you've got to put things into words that the public will understand.

SW: simple

DK: in your heart of hearts you must realise sometimes that's not actually the right thing to say … but it's the only way you can put it over if you've got to get it over in two minutes or three minutes

SW: did you actually write that section which refers to the 45 minutes Or was it somebody else?

DK: errr. I didn't write THAT section, no. I mean I reviewed the whole thing, I was involved with the whole process … In the end it was just a flurry of activity and it was very difficult to get comments in because people at the top of the ladder didn't want to hear some of the things

SW: so you expressed your unease about it? Put it that way

DK: errr well … yes yep yes

SW: so how do you feel now number ten is furiously denying it and Alastair Campbell specifically saying it's all nonsense it was all in the intelligence material?

DK: well I think it's matter of perception isn't it. I think people will perceive things and they'll be, how shall I put it, they'll see it from their own standpoint and they may not even appreciate quite what they were doing

SW: do you think there ought to be a security and intelligence committee inquiry?

DK: yes but not now. I think that has to be done in about six months time when we actually have come to the end of the evaluation of Iraq and the information that is going to come out of it. I still think it's far too early to be talking about the intelligence that is there ... a lot of intelligence that would appear to be good quality intelligence, some of which is not and it take a long long time to get the information that's required from Iraq. The process has only just started. I think one of the problems with dossier - and again I think you and I have talked about it in the past is that it was presented in a very black and white way without any sort of quantitative aspects of it. The only quantitative aspects were the figures derived essentially from UNSCOM figures, which in turn are Iraq's figures presented to UNSCOM - you know the xxx litres anthrax, the 4 tonnes VX - all of that actually is Iraqi figures - but there was nothing else in there that was quantitative or even remotely qualitative - I mean it was just a black and white thing - they have weapons or they don't have weapons. That in turn has been interpreted as being a vast arsenal and I'm not sure any of us ever said that .... people have said to me that that was what was implied, Again we discussed it ... and I discussed it with many people, that my own perception is that yes they have weapons but actually not xzxxxx (xxx not problem) at this point in time. The PROBLEM was that one could anticipate that without any form of inspection, and that forms a real deterrence, other than the sanctions side of things, then that that would develop. I think that was the real concern that everyone had, it was not so much what they have now but what they would have in the future. But that unfortunately wasn't expressed strongly in the dossier because that takes away the case for war ... (I cough) to a certain extent

SW: a clear and present, imminent threat?

DK: yes

...

SW: ok ... just back momentarily on the 45 minute issue ... I'm feeling like I ought to just explore that a little bit more with you ... the um ... err So would it be accurate then, as you did in that earlier conversation, to say that it was Alastair Campbell himself who ...?

DK: No I can't. All I can say is the Number Ten press office. I've never met Alastair Campbell so I can't ... (SW interrupts: they seized on that?) But ... I think Alastair Campbell is synonymous with that press office because he's responsible for it.

On 31 May 2003 on the Today programme Mr Gilligan broadcast the following report which was introduced as 'The Andrew Gilligan Essay':

> In show biz they say you should never work with children or animals. In politics, may be the rule should be never work with children, animals or dossiers.

> On Iraq, Tony Blair has issued three and they've all been questioned. The one on Saddam's security apparatus, famously largely copied of (sic) the internet. The one criticising Iraq's human rights record, which achieved the unusual feat for something on that subject of being attacked by Amnesty International. But it's the first, and the most substantial of the dossiers that's now, potentially, the most troublesome.

> The first mention of it was on the 25th February 2002. A BBC poll had shown that 86 out [of] 100 Labour backbenchers didn't think there was enough evidence of the threat posed by Saddam. The dossier would, it was promised, provide that evidence. It was written during March; publication was promised for the end of the month but was shelved. The Government said it didn't want to alarm people. The papers said that it

was because the dossier wasn't alarming enough. The BBC's intelligence and technical sources agreed. They told us that it didn't add much to what any well-informed layman already knew.

'What you have to understand is that 10 to 15 years ago, there was a lot of information. With a concealment and deception operation by the Iraqis, there's far less material.'

Other media heard the same. On August 29th, senior Whitehall sources told Michael Evans, Defence Editor of the *Times*, that the dossier was 'not revelatory'. On September 2nd, a Whitehall source told Richard Norton-Taylor, Security Editor of the *Guardian*: 'The dossier will no longer play a role. There's very little new to put in it.'

The very next morning, however, Mr Blair announced that the dossier would after all be published, and it was, on September 24th. By that day, the dossier, described as unrevelatory only 4 weeks before, had suddenly become very revelatory indeed. A senior figure involved in compiling it, told this programme two days ago that Downing Street had applied pressure to make it sexier. This quote from a British official appeared in yesterday's Washington Post:

'They were pressured and super-heated debates between Downing Street officials and intelligence officials over the contents of the dossier.'

The Prime Minister and his staff have spent the last two days denying claims that nobody has actually ever made, such as that material from the dossier was invented; that it came from sources other than the intelligence agencies; and that Downing Street wrote the dossier. They have, however, failed to deny several of the claims which the BBC source did make. There's been no denial of his allegation that the dossier was re-written the week before publication, nor has there been any denial that the line about Iraq's 45 minute deployment of biological weapons was added to the dossier at a late stage. When we put both these questions to Downing Street, they replied that they refused to discuss processology.

On both sides of the Atlantic, relations between intelligence professionals and their political masters are at a low ebb. In Washington, retired spies have written to President Bush saying the American public was misled. In Britain we've now seen two unprecedented intelligence leaks, directly challenging the Prime Minister. Time, perhaps, to take stock.

On 1 June 2003 The Mail on Sunday published an article written by Mr Gilligan. The first two columns of the first page of the article carried a photograph of Mr Alastair Campbell (the Prime Minister's Director of Communications) with a smaller photograph of Mr Gilligan below with the words in the nature of a headline:

I asked my intelligence source why Blair misled us all over Saddam's WMD. His response? One word ... CAMPBELL

In the article Mr Gilligan wrote (inter alia):

The location was a central London hotel and the source was waiting as I got there. We'd both been too busy to meet for nearly a year, but there was no sign this would be anything more than a routine get-together.

We started off by moaning about the railways. Only after about half-an-hour did the story emerge that would dominate the headlines for 48 hours, ruin Tony Blair's Basra awayday and work the Prime Minister into a state of controlled fury.

The source agreed with Blair about one thing. He, too, was adamant that Iraq had had a Weapons of Mass Destruction programme in the recent past. He pointed out some tell-tale signs that the chief UN weapons inspector, Hans Blix, seemed to have missed. But he knew, better than anyone, that it didn't amount to the 'imminent threat' touted by Ministers.

And he was gently despairing about the way No.10 had spoiled its case by exaggeration. 'Typical Downing Street', he said, half smiling, half annoyed.

We'd discussed the famous Blair dossier on Iraq's weapons at our previous meeting, a few months before it was published last September. 'It's really not very exciting, you know,' he'd told me. So what, I asked him now, had changed?

'Nothing changed', he said. 'Until the week before, it was just like I told you. It was transformed the week before publication, to make it sexier.'

What do you mean? Can I take notes? 'The classic', he said 'was the statement that WMD were ready for use in 45 minutes. One source said it took 45 minutes to launch a missile and that was misinterpreted to mean that WMD could be deployed in 45 minutes. There was no evidence that they had loaded conventional missiles with WMD, or could do so anything like that quickly.'

I asked him how this transformation happened. The answer was a single word. 'Campbell'.

What? Campbell made it up? 'No, it was real information. But it was included against our wishes because it wasn't reliable.'

On 2 June 2003 in the BBC Newsnight programme at 10.30pm Ms Susan Watts broadcast a report in relation to the September dossier. The transcript of the relevant part of the Newsnight programme is as follows:
SW: Over the weekend the storm over the missing weapons of mass destruction focused down on one key point: was the British public duped over the

urgency of dealing with Iraq's banned weapons? The government's claim that Saddam could mobilise these within forty five minutes is already looking shaky, but on the Today programme this morning the Foreign Secretary, Jack Straw, suggested it had never been a key part of the argument.

JACK STRAW: If you look at for example the key speech that the Prime Minister made on the 18th of March before the House of Commons, from my quick re-reading of it this morning, I can for example find no reference to this now famous forty five minutes.

SW: But the reference to forty five minutes was there in the Prime Minister's speech to the Commons on the day he published his famous weapons dossier.

TONY BLAIR: It concludes that Iraq has chemical and biological weapons, that Saddam has continued to produce them, that he has existing and active military plans for the use of chemical and biological weapons, which could be activated within forty five minutes including against his own Shia population.

SW: And it features in the dossier itself four times, notably in the Prime Minister's forward and the executive summary.

SW: Today, at the GH (sic) summit in Evian, Tony Blair once again found himself in rebuttal mode.

TONY BLAIR: The idea that we doctored such intelligence is completely and totally false, every single piece of intelligence that we presented was cleared very properly by the Joint Intelligence Committee.

SW: It's a surprising claim to make given that it encompasses the other so called dodgy dossier, part of which was plagiarised, and in any case today Tony Blair appeared irritated that the weapons issue won't go away.

TONY BLAIR: I think it is important that if people actually have evidence, they produce it, but it is wrong frankly for people to make allegations on the basis of so called anonymous sources when the facts are precisely the facts that we've stated.

SW: But in some cases anonymous sources could be the only way to gain an insight into the intelligence world. We've spoken to a senior official intimately involved with the process of pulling together the original September 2002 Blair weapons' dossier. We cannot name this person because their livelihood depends on anonymity. Our source made clear that in the run up to publishing the dossier the government was obsessed with finding intelligence on immediate Iraqi threats and the government's insistence the Iraqi threat was imminent was a Downing Street interpretation of intelligence conclusions. His point is that, while the intelligence community was agreed on the potential Iraqi threat in the future, there was less agreement about the threat the Iraqis posed at that moment. Our source said:

SOURCE: That was the real concern, not so much what they had now but what they would have in the future, but that unfortunately was not expressed strongly in the dossier, because that takes away the case for war to a certain extent. But in the end it was just a flurry of activity and it was very difficult to get comments in because people at the top of the ladder didn't want to hear some of the things.

SW: Our source talks of a febrile atmosphere in the days of diplomacy leading to the big Commons debate of September last year; of the government seizing on anything useful to the case, including the possibly (sic) existence of weapons that could be ready within forty five minutes.

SOURCE: It was a statement that was made it just got out of all proportion. They were desperate for information, they were pushing hard for information that could be released. That was one that popped up and it was seized on, and it's unfortunate that it was. That's why there is the argument between the intelligence services and Cabinet Office number 10, because they picked up on it, and once they've picked up on it you can't pull it back from them.

SW: And again, specifically on the forty five minute point:

SOURCE: It was in (sic) interesting week before the dossier was put out because there were so many people saying 'well I'm not so sure about that', or in fact they were happy with it being in, but not expressed the way that it was, because the word-smithing is actually quite important. The intelligence community are a pretty cautious lot on the whole but once you get people presenting it for public consumption then of course they use different words.

SW: The problem is that the forty five minutes point was not corroborated. For sceptics it highlights the dangers of relying too heavily on information from defectors. Journalists in America are being accused of running propaganda from the Iraqi National Congress.

The Foreign Affairs Select Committee (FAC) is a Committee of Members of Parliament appointed by the House of Commons to examine the expenditure, administration and policy of the FCO and its associated public bodies. On 3 June 2003 the FAC announced that it would hold an inquiry into 'The Decision to go to War in Iraq'. The announcement stated:

> The inquiry will consider whether the Foreign and Commonwealth Office, within the Government as a whole, presented accurate and complete information to Parliament in the period leading up to military action in Iraq, particularly in relation to Iraq's weapons of mass destruction. The Committee will hear oral evidence from several witnesses in June and will report to the House in July.

In his evidence Mr Donald Anderson MP, the Chairman of the FAC, stated that Mr Gilligan's 'revelations' in the Today programme were part of the context in which the Committee's decision to hold an inquiry was taken.

On 4 June 2003 Sir Kevin Tebbit wrote to the Chief of Defence Intelligence about the intense level of concern in respect of leaks or unauthorised statements made to journalists by members of the intelligence services or those close to them:

We spoke about this in the margins of the COS meeting this morning. There is clearly an intense level of high level concern about leaks or unauthorised statements made to journalists by members of the intelligence services or those close to them. While I have no reason to suspect anyone from the DIS, it is important that we do all we can to be satisfied that this is the case, and to remind staff of their professional obligations.

2. I discussed this with Sir David Omand last night and would be grateful if you could ensure that the following action is taken:

a notice to all staff (however discreetly handled) to report to you any suspicions as to the identity of any leaker. Of particular concern will be anyone known to be unhappy about the use made of the intelligence about '45 minute' WMD readiness. Please report any findings to me in the first instance;

any information we have about particular known contacts in the MOD;

a reminder to staff of the need to observe confidentiality in line with their professional obligations and to report any concerns about the use of intelligence to the management/command chain only;

3. I stress that I do not have any specific suspicions of the DIS. The information in the press is so generalised that it could have come from a much wider group, beyond DIS and the Agencies. For that reason, neither Sir David Omand nor I believe a formal leak inquiry is indicated, certainly at this stage. But we need to do all we can to investigate and tighten up.

4. As we discussed, DCDI may be the best person to handle this, particularly given Martin Howard's past experience as DGCC.

On 4 June 2003 in the BBC Newsnight programme at 10.30pm Ms Susan Watts broadcast a further report relating to the September dossier. The transcript of the relevant part of the programme is as follows:

SW: The questions for any inquiry are piling up. First, how sound was the Government's assertion that Saddam could launch banned weapons at 45 minutes' notice. The issue dominated today's debate. Tony Blair flatly denied that the 45-minute claim had unsettled the intelligence services.

TONY BLAIR: The claim about 45 minutes provoked disquiet amongst the intelligence community who disagreed with its inclusion in the dossier. Again, this is something I've discussed again with the chairman of the Joint Intelligence Committee. That allegation also is completely and totally untrue.

SW: But a source we've spoken to, a senior official intimately involved with the process of pulling together the original weapons dossier in which the claim was made, told us that he and others felt considerable discomfort over it.

ACTOR'S VOICE: I was uneasy with it. My problem was I could give other explanations which I've indicated to you, that it was the time to erect something like a Scud missile or it's the time to full a multi-barrel rocket launcher. All sorts of reasons why 45 minutes might well be important.

SW: In other words he is saying that Saddam might have rocket hardware that takes 45 minutes to assemble but not necessarily the weapons of mass destruction to which Tony Blair referred in his weapons dossier, when he said of Saddam: The document discloses that his military planning allows for some of the WMD to be ready within 45 minutes of an order to use them. The Prime Minister appeared to want to shift the focus of the argument, moving away from how the 45 minute claim was used to who put it in the weapons dossier.

TONY BLAIR: .... including the judgment about the so-called 45 minutes was a judgment made by the Joint Intelligence Committee and by them alone.

SW: Our source was not disputing that the 45-minute assessment was included in the dossier by the intelligence services although he did say he felt that to have been a mistake. His point was that the emphasis placed on that element of the intelligence in the foreword to the dossier went too far. He felt this emphasis turned a possible capability into an imminent threat and a critical part of the Government's case for war. Our source cannot be described as a rogue element. On the contrary, he is exceptionally well placed to judge the prevailing mood as the dossier of September last year was put together.

On 19 June 2003 Mr Gilligan gave evidence to the FAC in relation to his reports in respect of the dossier on the Today programme on 29 May 2003. In his evidence he stated that these reports were based on a single source but he did not identify this source.

On 25 June Mr Alastair Campbell gave evidence in relation to the September dossier to the FAC. In the course of his evidence he said that it was untrue for the BBC to allege that the Prime Minister took the country into military conflict on the basis of a lie and he further said:

> ...the story that I 'sexed up' the dossier is untrue: the story that I 'put pressure on the intelligence agencies' is untrue: the story that we somehow made more of the 45 minute command and control point than the intelligence agencies thought was suitable is untrue.

# CHAPTER 3

On 30 June 2003 Dr Kelly wrote a letter to Dr Bryan Wells, his line manager in the MoD. Dr Wells held the post of Director of Counter Proliferation and Arms Control in the MoD. The letter was received by Dr Wells in the late afternoon of 1 July. The letter was as follows:

> Over the past month controversy has raged over the September 2002 Iraq WMD Dossier primarily because Andrew Gilligan of the BBC has claimed that the dossier was 'sexed up' at the behest of Alastair Campbell the Prime Minister's press officer.
>
> Andrew Gilligan is a journalist that I know and have met.
>
> As you know I have been involved in writing three 'dossiers' concerning Iraq – the 1999 UNSCOM/Butler Status of Verification Report, the September 2002 International Institute of Strategic Studies 'Iraq WMD' report, and the UK Government 'Iraq's Weapons of Mass Destruction'. My contributions to the latter were in part 2 (History of UN Inspections) and part 1 chapter 2 (Iraq's programmes 1971–1998) at the behest of the FCO and I was not involved in the intelligence component in any way nor in the process of the dossier's compilation. I have not acknowledged to anyone outside FCO my contribution to any [of] these reports although it is easy to assume and conclude that I made contributions because of my substantial role in elucidating Iraq's biological weapons programme. I am not a member of the intelligence community although I interact with that community and I am essentially, as an inspector, a consumer of intelligence not a generator of intelligence.
>
> The contents of both IISS and UK Government dossiers, which both rely heavily on the 1999 Butler report, I have discussed with many indi-

viduals drawn from the UN, 'Think Tanks' academia, the arms control community, together with the media. My discussions have been entirely technical and factual and although the '45 minute deployment' issue has obviously been raised I have always given the honest answer that I do not know what it refers to and that I am not familiar with an Iraqi weapons system that it matches. The latter is of significance to the UN since they had to take it into account in their work. The UK Dossier was of general interest for about ten days after publication and, with the exception of UNMOVIC, was not a topic later raised with me. After that my discussions about Iraq's WMD centred on UNMOVIC's re–engagement with Iraq, the 'enhanced' inspection process and UNVMOVIC's findings. Since the war I have discussed with some of those same individuals the failure to use chemical and biological weapons by Iraq and the apparent lack of success in finding such weapons after the war. It is natural to do so since I am one of the few who knows Iraq's programmes in detail and my information is derived from my United Nations work.

I have not had extensive dealings with Andrew Gilligan. As I recall I first met him at the IISS 'Global Strategic Review' in September 2002 after the IISS dossier was published but before the UK Government dossier appeared. We would have discussed the IISS dossier since it was at the forefront of delegates discussions but the detail is now forgotten. I cannot recall meeting him before that although it is entirely possible that we have attended the same meetings at Chatham House or IISS. I next met with him in February 2003 at his request because he was about to depart to Iraq to cover the forthcoming war. I cannot recall any contact in the interim and do not believe that contact was made. It is some time since that meeting but I believe that we covered the topics of Hans Blix and UNMOVIC inspections, Iraqi individuals associated with the WMD programmes and sites associated with the programme. I also spoke separately with Linsey Hilsum (Channel 4), Carolyn Hawley and Jane Corbin (BBC) about the same issues before they went to Iraq. Gilligan said that he would informally tell me about his experiences in Iraq on his return (as did Jane Corbin). I have spoken to both since the war.

I have had a number of telephone exchanges with Jane Corbin principally because she is keen to do a follow up to her UNMOVIC 'fly on the wall' with the Iraq Survey Group (and my comments to her have been neutral) but none with Gilligan other than one made by him to arrange to meet to discuss his experience in Iraq. I also speak irregularly with Susan Watts the BBC Science Editor and Andrew Veitch the Channel Four Science Editor about scientific and technical aspects of Iraq's weapons and UN inspections.

I met with Gilligan in London on May 22nd for 45 minutes in the evening to privately discuss his Iraq experiences and definitely not to discuss the dossier (I would not have met with him had it been the case). As I recall, we discussed his ability to report before, during, and after the war in the presence of minders and freedom to move around Baghdad; accommodation at the Palestine Hotel; his impression of the coalition attacks; US military protection of journalists; the revelations likely to be made by Amer Al-Sa'adi, Huda Amash, Rihab Taha, Tariq Aziz and Ahmed Murtadda who are individuals associated with Iraq's 'past' programme. He was particularly intrigued by Huda since he visited her home and met her husband but not Huda after the war and found her home guarded by 'regime' Iraqis. We also discussed the failure of Iraq to use WMD and the inability to find them. I offered my usual and standard explanations (conditions early in the war not favourable to CB use and lack of command and control late in the war; that the small arsenal of weapons (or its destroyed remnants) compared to 1991 would be difficult to find without human information). The issue of 45 minutes arose in terms of the threat (aerial versus land launch) and I stated that I did not know what it refers to (which I do not). He asked why it should be in the dossier and I replied probably for impact. He raised the issue of Alastair Campbell and since I was not involved in the process (not stated by me) I was unable to comment. This issue was not discussed at any length and was essentially an aside. I made no allegations or accusations about any issue related to the dossier or the Government's case for war concentrating on his account of his stay in Iraq. I did not discuss the 'immediacy' of the threat. The discussion was not about the dossier. Had it been so then I would have indicated that from my extensive and authoritative knowledge of Iraq's WMD programme, notably its biological programme, that the dossier was a fair reflection of open source information (ie UNSCOM/UNMOVIC) and appreciations.

I most certainly have never attempted to undermine Government policy in any way especially since I was personally sympathetic to the war because I recognised from a decade's work the menace of Iraq's ability to further develop its non-conventional weapons programmes.

I have had no further contact with Andrew Gilligan since May 22nd.

I did not even consider that I was the 'source' of Gilligan's information until a friend in RUSI said that I should look at the 'Oral Evidence provided to the Foreign Affairs Committee' on 19th June because she recognised that some comments were the sort that I would make about Iraq's chemical and biological capacity. The description of that meeting in small part matches my interaction with him especially my personal evaluation of Iraq's capability but the overall character is quite different. I can only conclude one of three things. Gilligan has considerably embellished my meeting with him; he has met with other individuals who truly were intimately associated with the dossier; or he has assembled comments from both multiple direct and indirect sources for his articles.

I should explain my 'unusual' interaction with the media. In August 1991 I led the first biological weapons inspection in Iraq. I had no media exposure before that although anticipating that it would be inevitable I attended at my request the MOD Senior Officers TV course at Wilton Park which served to make me aware of some of the pitfalls of journalism. During and after the first inspection as Chief Inspector I conducted a number of major press conferences including the internationally covered midday press briefing at UN Headquarters in New York. That meant that the media were very much aware of me thereafter. Over the next ten years I undertook at the request of MOD, FCO, CBD Porton Down, and the (sic) especially the UN press office and UNSCOM/UNMOVIC press officer both attributable interviews and occasionally unattributable briefings. All such interactions were cleared by the appropriate authority. As my contact details became known it became inevitable that direct approaches were made and I used my discretion as [to] whether I provided information. My interaction with the media helped keep the issue of Iraq's WMD a live issue. I interact with the media on four issues – Iraq, Soviet/Russian biological warfare, smallpox and anthrax. If it was technical information available from open sources (and nearly all requests were such) then I provided details or more real-istically a clarification and explanation of that information (I tend to be a human archive on Iraq's chemical and biological programmes). If it was about individuals (Iraqi or UN) I would comment only on their role and not their personality. Comment on other matters were declined although in the case of Iraq it is impossible to draw a clear distinction between the truly technical and Iraq's political concealment.

I have appeared on many British and foreign television programmes including Today, Panorama, Channel 4 News, Newsnight, ABC, CBS sixty minutes, CNN etc. and I continue to get requests to do so. Since September 11th I no longer talk to camera about Iraq and rarely on other issues. All media requests are referred to James Paver of the FCO Press Office and most are now discouraged from approaching him by my stating that I doubted that it would be possible.

I have never served as a designated spokesperson for any organisa-tion, never initiated the release of information on behalf of any organi-sation, and never discussed a JIC report. I have never contacted any journalist to claim that a newspaper report was correct (or incorrect). I have never made a claim as to the timing of when any part of the dossier was included. I have never acted as a conduit to release or leak information. I have never discussed classified information with anyone other than those cleared so to do. I do not feel 'deep unease' over the dossier because it is completely coincident with my personal views on Iraq's unconventional weapons capability.

With hindsight I of course deeply regret talking to Andrew Gilligan even though I am convinced that I am not his primary source of infor-mation. At the time of considerable disarray in Iraq I was eager to gain whatever first hand information I could about the circumstances in Iraq and individuals associated with Iraq's WMD programme. I anticipated, incorrectly, that I would shortly return to Iraq to debrief some of those individuals and this is why I have spoken to some journalists who have also interacted with them recently.

I hope this letter helps unravel at least a small part of the '45 minute story'. It was a difficult decision to make to write to you because I realise that suspicion falls on me because of my long association with Iraq's WMD programme investigation and the acknowledgement that I know Andrew Gilligan. I can only repeat that I do not believe that I am the single source referred to and that much of the information attributed to that source I am completely unsighted on and would not be able to provide informed comment about.

On 2 July Dr Wells wrote to Mr Martin Howard, the Deputy Chief of Defence Intelligence:

You will wish to be aware of the attached letter that David Kelly has sent me. I am planning to speak to David about it on the afternoon of 4 July, and would welcome the opportunity to discuss with you before-hand. You may wish to pass a copy to the leak inquiry personnel.

Mr Howard received Dr Wells' letter on 3 July and he informed Sir Kevin Tebbit of Dr Wells' letter and of Dr Wells' intention to speak to Dr Kelly on the afternoon of 4 July. Sir Kevin then decided that Dr Kelly should be interviewed by Mr Richard Hatfield, the Personnel Director of the MoD together with Dr Wells. Sir Kevin also informed the Secretary of State for Defence, Mr Geoffrey Hoon MP, that an official, whom he did not name, had admitted speaking to Mr Gilligan and that he would be interviewed the next day.

On 4 July Mr Hatfield interviewed Dr Kelly at 11.30am and Dr Wells also attended the interview. On 7 July Mr Hatfield prepared a note of the interview. The note was as follows:

I interviewed Dr Kelly about his letter dated 30 June to his line manager, Dr Bryan Wells, at 11.30 on Friday 4 July. Dr Wells was present. The interview ended at approximately 13:15.

I began by explaining to Dr Kelly that his letter had serious implications. First, on the basis of his own account, it appeared that he breached the normal standards of Civil Service behaviour and departmental regulations by having had a number of unauthorised and unreported contacts with journalists. Regardless of the detail of what had passed, this opened up the possibility of disciplinary action. Second, his unauthorised discussion with Andrew Gilligan on 22 May appeared to be directly relevant to the controversy surrounding allegations made by Gilligan about the government's WMD dossier even if, as he had said in his letter, this had not been the discussion described by Gilligan at the FAC hearing.

I had two objects in the interview. First, I was looking to form a view of whether there was evidence to suggest that a sufficiently serious offence might have been committed to warrant formal disciplinary action. If I so concluded, the next step would be to initiate a formal fact-finding hearing in accordance with departmental procedures at which he could be accompanied by a colleague or TU representative if he so wished. Alternatively, I might conclude that a lesser offence had been committed which could be dealt with informally or that no offence had been committed. Second, I wished to try to establish if his meeting with Andrew Gilligan was likely to form the basis of evidence given by Gilligan to the FAC about the WMD dossier.

Dr Kelly said that he understood this.

I then asked him briefly to clarify one or two points in his letter which were not entirely clear before asking him to explain more fully the account on the second page of his dealings with journalists.

Dr Kelly said that he was widely known as an expert on Iraqi WMD, not least because of his extensive experience as a UN inspector. During his period with the UN he had often been asked to act as an expert spokesman. Subsequently, he continued to participate in many seminars and similar events concerning this and related subjects. He was often approached by academics, journalists and others operating in the field for background information and technical advice at such events and, sometimes, outside them. When a journalist approached him, he usually consulted the FCO press office, but on occasions he used his own judgment as explained in his letter.

I asked why he consulted the FCO press office rather [than] the MOD. Dr Kelly said that his salary was paid by the FCO. I said that was irrelevant – he was seconded to MOD. I asked who had given him authority to exercise his own judgment about contacts with journalists on defence related business, since this was contrary to standing departmental instructions. Dr Kelly said that he had never read those instructions, nor sought to discover what guidance existed about contact with journalists. He said that he had not really regarded his discussions [with] journalists, academics etc as being about defence business but as a continuation of his role as UN expert. I said that that was, at best, extraordinarily naïve – journalists were not seeking information out of academic interest but to construct stories. It was important to know the context of their enquiries and any particular sensitivities before speaking to them. I asked Dr Kelly whether, for example, he knew that one of the other journalists to whom he had spoken, was married to a member of the FAC. He said he did not. This was an illustration of why people were required to seek advice and permission from the press office before speaking to journalists. It was also very important to report back after contacts.

I then asked Dr Kelly to summarise his contacts with Gilligan. He said that he had first met and spoken to Gilligan at the IISS seminar on WMD in September 2002 which took place just before publication of the government dossier. He was unaware of having spoken to Gilligan previously, although it was possible that they might both [have] been at other similar events without being aware of each other. Gilligan had telephoned in February 2003 to say that he was going to Iraq and would like to meet for some background briefing. I asked Dr Kelly why, given that there was an interval of 24 hours before the meeting, he had not contacted even the FCO press office. He said that he had regarded it as non-sensitive because it was the sort of background that he would have given to any academic or journalist.

Dr Kelly said his next contact with Gilligan was in May. Gilligan rang him to offer feedback from his experiences in Iraq. He had accepted, for the reasons set out in his letter. They met on 22 May in the Charing Cross Hotel. [Dr Kelly later said that the meeting took place about 1745 and lasted until approx 1830]. Gilligan took notes but did not appear to have a tape recorder (although Kelly did not ask and there was no discussion of the basis of the meeting). The vast bulk of the conversation was about Iraqi individuals associated with WMD programmes, the course of the war, and why WMD had not been used. In the course of the latter, as recorded in his letter, Gilligan had raised the reference in the September dossier to the possibility of weapons being deployed in 45 minutes. Kelly had commented that this did not correspond with any weapon system that he knew. Gilligan had asked why he thought the claim had been included in the dossier. Kelly had said that he had assumed that it was for impact. Although he did not know what the claim was based on, it emphasised the immediacy of the threat. [I have prepared a detailed comparison of Kelly's account of his conversation with Gilligan's FAC evidence based on the second part of the interview.] I asked why he had not even reported the conversation afterwards, given the public debate about the two government dossiers. Kelly repeated that the discussion had not really been about the dossier and he had not said anything controversial. Indeed, even after Gilligan made his allegations, he had not made any association with their May 22 meeting. It was only when a colleague remarked to him that some of the comments attributed to Gilligan's source sounded similar to his own views that he realised that others might make similar connections, which was why he had written to his line manager. As he had said in his letter, however, he did not believe that he could be Gilligan's primary source because he had not made any allegations against the government and his views also differed from those attributed to the source in other ways.

At this point I asked Dr Kelly whether he was confident that he had accurately reflected the meeting with Gilligan and whether there was anything he had omitted about this other meetings (sic). I stressed that whatever the actual significance of anything he had said to Gilligan, their meeting could turn out to be very important in relation to the public dispute between the government and the BBC about Gilligan's claims. It might become necessary to consider a public statement based on his account. Gilligan's reputation was at stake and he would be bound to challenge any inaccuracies – and I reminded Dr Kelly of the possibility that he might have been tape–recorded. Dr Kelly said that he understood this but stood by his account.

I said that I was prepared to accept his account in good faith. On the basis of what his letter and what he had said, it was clear that he had breached departmental instructions on numerous occasions by having conversations with journalists which had been neither unauthorised (sic) by or reported to the MOD press office, although on most occasions he had consulted the FCO press office. His contact with Gilligan was particularly ill–judged. Even if he was not Gilligan's primary source, it had had very awkward consequences both for him and the department, much of which could have been avoided even if he had reported the contact immediately afterwards. Someone who had dealt regularly with the press in a previous capacity should have known better. This was a potentially very serious matter. Nevertheless, I accepted his assurance that there has been no malicious intent and there appeared no reason to believe that classified material had been revealed. On that basis, I judged that it would not be appropriate to initiate formal disciplinary proceedings. I would, however, write to him shortly to record my displeasure at his conduct. I went on to instruct him to familiarise himself with departmental guidance about dealings with the media, to report all contacts to his line manager and never to agree to an interview without explicit authority. Finally, I warned Dr Kelly that any further breaches would be almost certain to lead to disciplinary action and the possibility of disciplinary action could of course be re–opened if further facts came to light that called his account and assurances into question.

The second part of the interview was devoted to a more detailed comparison of Dr Kelly's interview with Gilligan's FAC appearance. I will summarise my conclusions – my detailed analysis is appended. (Dr Wells also took notes.)

It is very difficult to reconcile Dr Kelly's account of his May 22 discussion with the evidence given to the FAC by Gilligan, if this is indeed all attributable to a single source. Kelly's account is consistent with some aspects of the FAC evidence and some of the discrepancies might be attributable to exaggeration, misrepresentation or misunderstanding by Gilligan and/or Kelly. Although Kelly admits to two comments that might lend credence to a claim that the dossier had been 'sexed–up', he denies making such a claim and the related allegations which Gilligan attributed to his 'single source' and Kelly was not involved in the preparation of the intelligence part of the dossier. The focus of the two discussions also appears different – the dossier is only a small part of the Kelly discussion and Kelly specifically denies telling Gilligan (or anyone else outside government) that he had had any involvement with the dossier. Moreover, some of the views attributed to the source appear directly contrary to those expressed by Kelly.

There is also some evidence that does point to the existence of a different source for these allegations. Some aspects of Gilligan's description of his source do not properly match Kelly (although exaggeration and misrepresentation to try to protect the identity of the source are both possible.). And, if Gilligan's answer to Q550 from the chairman is accurate, the source is a member of the intelligence services, which cannot be a description of Kelly. Another serious discrepancy is that both Gilligan's FAC evidence and the original article suggest that he had a discussion with his source in May 2002, several months before he met Kelly.

Gilligan refers to four sources in the FAC session. There does not have to be a fifth person. It is possible that there is no single source and that the allegations are a collage, to which Kelly's interview contributed but the specific allegations about interference with the dossier come from somewhere else. Another possibility is that there are really only

53

three sources: the 'single source' might actually be one of the other three sources referred to by Gilligan as providing different information.

If both Gilligan's and Kelly's accounts are essentially truthful, perhaps the most likely supposition is that Kelly appeared to provide broad collateral for Gilligan's 'single source' claims about the dossier, although not for the specific allegations about political interference. During his FAC hearing Gilligan talks about the 'single source' as the centre of his 45–minute story but comments that this is supported by other evidence.

Dr Wells prepared a note of the interview on 4 July which was as follows:

Present:
Mr Richard Hatfield, Personnel Director
Dr Bryan Wells, DCPAC
Dr David Kelly, CPAC Special Adviser

1. Hatfield said that he wanted to go through the Transcript of Gilligan's evidence to the Foreign Affairs Committee and ask Kelly whether he could have been the source of what Gilligan said. He went through Gilligan's answers seriatim.

2. Q398 answer. Hatfield observed that Gilligan's meeting with his source might match his meeting with Kelly. In particular, the meeting had been Gilligan's initiative, and the source was quite closely connected with the issue of Iraqi WMD. Hatfield acknowledged that Kelly's account did not match Gilligan's descriptions of the source as someone he had known for some time, and that he had met several times and spoken on the phone from time to time; but Gilligan could have been embellishing.

3. Q417. Hatfield observed that the description of the source as a 'British official who was involved in the preparation of the Dossier' matched Kelly. Kelly accepted this, but said that he had never acknowledged his

role in the Dossier to anyone outside Government, although some might have guessed.

4. Q418 answer. Hatfield observed that the description of the source as 'longstanding' and 'one of the senior officials in charge of drawing up the Dossier' did not match Kelly, but again Gilligan could have been exaggerating.

5. Q449. Hatfield asked direct if Kelly had ever said that the '45 minute' assessment was put into the Dossier at a late stage (ie the week before publication, as Gilligan had alleged). Kelly replied that he had not been aware of the assessment (that some of Iraq's WMD could be ready within 45 minutes of an order) until he read it in the published version of the Dossier. He had not been involved in the final preparations of the Dossier (he had not been in London during August, but had been in September). The only late issue he had been involved in was responding to a request on whether from his perspective there was anything else to add to the Dossier. He had suggested adding passages on smallpox, but this had not been taken up. Hatfield double-checked – Kelly was saying that he was not aware of the 45 minute assessment until it was published and had no knowledge of the process by which it had been brought into the Dossier. Kelly confirmed.

6. Q451 answer. Hatfield asked again if Kelly was the source of the 'allegations' about the sexing-up of the Dossier. Kelly replied that he was not.

7. Q453 answer. Hatfield asked if Kelly had discussed (he had) (sic) discussed with Gilligan the issue of Uranium being sought from Niger. Kelly said he thought he had, but he was not involved in the issue and would not have offered his own view (his own position was that he had nothing other than the IAEA view). Hatfield asked again in relation to Q454 answer: Kelly replied that he did not (and would not have) offered the view that this assessment was based on 'unreliable information'.

8. Q455. Hatfield asked again if Kelly had been the source of the allegations about the '45 minute claim'. Kelly reiterated that he was not.

9. Q457 answer. Hatfield asked if there had been an exchange in which he identified Alastair Campbell as the person from No.10 who had asked for the Dossier to be changed to include the '45 minute claim'. Kelly said that he had not said anything like the quotation that Gilligan attributed to the source: he did not have 'wishes' in relation to the contents of the Dossier.

10.Q461 answer. Hatfield asked if the source's quote (that the '45 minute claim' had confused conventional and CBW deployment times) reflected Kelly's views. Kelly replied that he had no opinion on the '45 minute claim'. He did not know what the original source was.

11. Q463 answer. Hatfield asked if Kelly shared the source's view that Downing Street had spoiled its case by exaggeration. Kelly replied that he had not said that the Dossier was exaggerated. He had taken the line that the threat from Iraqi WMD was current and specific.

12. Q478. Hatfield observed that Kelly had already denied alleging that the 45 minute claim was unreliable.

13. Q486 answer. Hatfield asked if Kelly shared the source's views that weapons at 45 minutes deployment would have been found by now because they could not be deeply concealed. Kelly replied that this was not a statement he would make.

14. Q511 answer. Hatfield asked if Kelly was of the view that Iraq had not been able to weaponise CBW. Kelly replied that this was not his assessment. Hatfield asked if Kelly shared the source's views that it was 30% likely that there had been an Iraqi CW programme in the 6 months before the conflict. Kelly replied that he had no doubt that Iraq had a CW programme, but this was the sort of assessment he might make

purely to weapons production. Hatfield probed: Gilligan was specifically quoting his source – had Kelly used those actual words? Kelly said that he had not, but accepted that it could be an inaccurate summation of what he might have said. Hatfield asked whether Kelly could have been the source of Gilligan's quotation in the Q545 answer (that it was more likely that Iraq had a BW programme, but that it was small). Kelly replied that he would not have used those terms, but that the statement could be a loose paraphrase of his views.

15. Q559. Hatfield observed that Kelly did not match Gilligan's confirmation that his source was someone in the intelligence services.

16. Q565 answer. Kelly observed that Gilligan's description of the meeting's duration as being 'a couple of hours, perhaps, an hour and a half' did not match the meeting he had been at: his strong recollection was that it had been around 45 minutes.

17. Hatfield summed up. There appeared to be consistencies between parts of Gilligan's testimony to the Foreign Affairs Committee, and what Kelly says that he said to Gilligan. In particular, the meeting was set up at Gilligan's initiative, and Kelly had acknowledged that the statement that it was 30% likely that there was a CW programme in the 6 months before the conflict was consistent with his views. But there were significant discrepancies. In particular, Kelly denied having any knowledge of the '45 minutes claim' until after the Dossier was published, and denied having any knowledge of the process by which that assessment was included; he also denied giving any opinion that the evidence that Uranium had been sought from Niger was based on unreliable information. In addition, Kelly was not of the view that Iraq had not been able to weaponise CBW. There were other, minor inconsistencies with Gilligan's testimony: Kelly had not met Gilligan 'several times', was not 'long–standing, well–known' to Gilligan, and was not in the intelligence services, but Gillian might well have wished to embellish. Hatfield said that overall, his judgment was that if there were a sin-

gle source for Gilligan's information, then it was not Kelly. Kelly's words may have been part of the background to Gilligan's stories, but on the basis of what he had testified, he was satisfied that Kelly was not the source of the most significant allegations.

On 4 July Sir Kevin Tebbit wrote to Sir David Omand, the Security and Intelligence Co-ordinator and Permanent Secretary of the Cabinet Office as follows:

An official in the MOD had volunteered that he had a discussion with Andrew Gilligan on 22 May, one week before Gilligan's allegation about the interference in the production of the September dossier and the '45 minute story'. He is an FCO official seconded to the MOD's Proliferation and Arms Control Secretariat, with a long history of authorised dealing with the press in the course of his duties, though not in this case.

He was interviewed today by his line manager and my Personnel Director for two hours. The official claims that he met Gilligan to discuss Gilligan's experiences in Baghdad because he believed it would be helpful to him in his own role as a BW expert with long scientific/academic association with the Iraqi weapons programme, past experience as a UN Inspector and an expectation that he would be returning to Iraq to debrief Iraqis associated with their WMD programme shortly. It would appear, from what he had told us, that their discussion touched on some of the issues subsequently referred to by Gilligan in the press in a number of ways:

in response to a question from Gilligan about the failure of Iraq to use WMD and the inability to find them, he said that conditions early in the war were not favourable and that there were command and control problems subsequently, and that the small arsenal of WMD remaining would be difficult to find without human information;

on the issue of the 45 minutes, raised by Gilligan, he said that he did not know to what it refers (not having access to the intelligence report);

asked why it should be in the dossier, he said that he replied 'probably for impact';

on the role of Alastair Campbell, he said he was unable to comment (not being involved in the process).

My immediate reaction was that this must be the 'single source' to whom Gilligan referred to in his testimony to the FAC as the origin of the story that the Government exaggerated intelligence contained in the September dossier. Certainly, his comments to Gilligan could have been incorporated into Gilligan's 29 May story. However, closer examination, following today's interview suggests that this would not necessarily be a reliable conclusion. A significant element of the information that Gilligan attributes to this source in his FAC testimony would not have been known to this individual: he was not, for example, involved in, or claims to have been involved in, the intelligence component of the dossier or the process of the dossier's compilation. There are also discrepancies, over the circumstances of the meeting, the length of their relationship, and, indeed, about the nature of the individual: Gilligan claims that this source was a senior official in charge of drawing up the dossier. This official – although an acknowledged expert on Iraqi WMD – patently was not so involved; nor does he subscribe to views attributed to Gilligan's source.

So, there are three possibilities:

(a) that Gilligan has embellished this official's meeting with him, but that he is the 'single anonymous source';

(b) that Gilligan's source is someone else;

(c) that no one 'source' exists and is in fact a hotchpotch of comments from numerous individuals and articles.

In the case of (a), we would have the strongest possible reason for publicly correcting the misrepresentation made by Gilligan in the interests of factual accuracy. However, we do not have sufficient evidence to reach such a conclusion with any degree of safety. The official himself is adamant that he is not the single source. Were we to accuse Gilligan and the BBC of misrepresenting the official's remarks, it would be easy for Gilligan to claim that his source was someone else and that the Government was pursuing a vendetta.

For these reasons, I do not recommend that we use what the official has told us to seek to correct the public record further.

I do, however, believe it necessary to have defensive material available should the story leak. Of this there must be a possibility. The official himself says he came forward, not because he considered that he was the source of Gilligan's information, but because a contact in RUSI suggested that Gilligan's evidence to the FAC looked as if it drew on the sort of comments he might make about Iraq's CW and BW capability. In general, there must, therefore, be some speculation already. Contingent lines have, therefore, been prepared by officials here. These are enclosed. [The contingent lines, which appear from the enclosure to the letter to have been a press statement, are set out in appendix 4].

I should add that the official has clearly breached the MOD's rules about unauthorised contact with the media. There is no reason to suspect a breach of the OSA [Official Secrets Act] or compromise of security information, but discipline is being reinforced.

I am copying this letter to Andrew Turnbull, David Manning (No.10), Michael Jay (FCO), Eliza Manningham-Buller (Security Services) and John Scarlett (JIC).

On the evening of Thursday 3 July Mr Hoon telephoned Mr Jonathan Powell, the Prime Minister's Chief of Staff and told him that an official had come forward to say that he had spoken to Mr Gilligan. Later on that evening in the course of a general conversation on the telephone with the Prime Minister, who was in the North West of England, Mr Powell passed on to the Prime Minister the information about an official having come forward. On the afternoon of Friday 4 July Sir David Manning, Head of the Overseas and Defence Secretariat of the Cabinet Office, held a meeting in his office in 10 Downing Street with Sir David Omand, Mr Powell and Mr John Scarlett, the Chairman of the Joint Intelligence Committee, to discuss the course of action which should be followed in light of the knowledge that an official had come forward to say that he had spoken to Mr Gilligan.

On 5 July Sir Kevin Tebbit sent a further letter to Sir David Omand in which he wrote:

> Since my letter to you yesterday afternoon, there has been a further development which points more strongly to our official as being the 'source' for the Gilligan allegation about the dossier (albeit with plenty of room still for the possibility of embellishment from other sources and misrepresentation by the journalist).
>
> Today's *Times* carries an article by Tom Baldwin which contains further hints as to Gilligan's informant. There are three new pointers, specifically:
>
> 'BBC journalists have been told that Mr Gilligan's anonymous source is among the 100 British intelligence and weapons specialists currently in Iraq as part of the ISG';
>
> 'Attempts to contact …. source in the past month to ask supplementary questions has proved unsuccessful because of the nature of his position';
>
> Asked if now based abroad the executive replied 'Something like that'.
>
> Although the official is not in Iraq at present I understand that he was there recently, after his conversation with Gilligan on 22 May and was planning to visit again later this month as an expert helping with the work of the Iraq Survey Group searching for WMD. The fact that the

BBC are uncertain of his precise whereabouts, is consistent with the official's statement at the MOD's interviews yesterday that he has had no contact with the BBC since 22 May. Gilligan will have been aware of his general plans to visit – the official states that this was the reason why he agreed to meet Gilligan in the first place – but the cutting of contact since then would explain the BBC's lack of precision in their knowledge about the exact timings of his presence in Iraq itself.

There remain many discrepancies between Gilligan's account of what he claims to have been told by the official and the official's own version of what transpired. We still cannot exclude the possibility that the main source, or other sources, are elsewhere. But it may be possible to explain and reconcile at least some of the mismatches. An official who denies having had access to the intelligence reporting or a hand in the production of the intelligence part of the dossier, as the official does, may nevertheless have said enough based on his expert knowledge of the earlier Iraqi programme, for someone of Gilligan's methods to claim that the official discredited the '45 minutes' intelligence eg by stating that such a high level of readiness did not correspond to the Iraqi systems of which he was aware.

Records of the MOD's interview with the official are still being prepared. I have asked that they be forwarded to us as soon as possible. But I wanted you and colleagues to be aware of this development immediately. The *Times* story today, whether accurate or not, will increase the likelihood that over the weekend other journalists will indeed identify and name the BBC's source as our official. (He is as I indicated in my earlier letter well known in media/academic circles).

There are also considerations, as we discussed yesterday, whether the Foreign Affairs Committee Chairman should be informed of what we now know, however inconclusive, before their report is published on Monday. And there is the question of whether this plays into the continuing impasse between the Government and the BBC.

I am copying this letter to Andrew Turnbull, David Manning (No.10), Michael Jay (FCO), Eliza Manningham–Buller (Security Service) and John Scarlett (JIC).

On 6 July Sir David Omand sent a letter to Sir Kevin Tebbit (dated 5 July) which Sir Kevin received on Monday 7 July in which Sir David wrote:

Thank you for your letter of Friday afternoon. I discussed the contents with Jonathan Powell, David Manning and John Scarlett that evening. We recognised that at least part of the explanation of the Gilligan story could rest on the discussion he had had with the official who has now come forward. At the appropriate point it would be incumbent upon us to inform the FAC (and the ISC) so that they were not placed in a false position. But we also noted your caveat about the need to be more certain of the facts before reaching any firm conclusion, given certain apparent discrepancies. The Prime Minister subsequently saw your letter and spoke to Jonathan Powell, and as I relayed to you, he agreed that as you had recommended no immediate action should be taken to try to correct the record with the FAC or with the BBC until we were more sure of our ground.

The Prime Minister asked for a deeper analysis of what the official has actually said, read against the account Gilligan himself has given the FAC and other statements by the BBC. You agreed to put this in hand, in the light of the record being prepared by Richard Hatfield. When we spoke later yesterday evening, we recognised that it might be necessary for the individual to be re-interviewed on Monday.

Your follow-up letter on Saturday has also been seen by the Prime Minister, who was grateful for the further information in it. He discussed the options with me on Sunday morning. I was able to pass on to him the view of the Foreign Secretary, relayed to me by the FCO Resident Clerk on Saturday evening, against any immediate action with the FAC in advance of the publication of their report on Monday (their Report is complete and some members of the Committee are now abroad). The Prime Minister concluded that notwithstanding the further circumstantial details in your second letter he agreed with your recommendation that there were still too many unknowns for us to approach the FAC now. But we may need to react quickly if the meeting of BBC Governors tonight or comment on the FAC Report changes the position. As I reported to you this afternoon the PM is appearing before the Liaison Committee on Tuesday and you will need to submit updated advice for that appearance in any case.

We agreed that you will circulate the detailed account of the first interview as soon as possible, and consider whether to reinterview the individual on Monday. I should add that the Prime Minister was minded to ask that the ISC be fully briefed in confidence on the case – the timing we can consider in the light of your further advice.

I am copying this letter to Andrew Turnbull, David Manning and Jonathan Powell, Eliza Manningham-Buller and John Scarlett, and to the Private Secretary to Michael Jay (whom you contacted yesterday).

In the course of Saturday and Sunday 5 and 6 July, a number of these senior officials had discussions on the telephone with each other as to the course which should be followed and some of them also had telephone conversations with the Prime Minister. In addition Mr Hoon and Mr Alastair Campbell had discussions on the telephone (see paragraph 307).

On the evening of Sunday 6 July at 6.30pm there was a special meeting of the BBC Governors to consider (inter alia) the issues arising from Mr Gilligan's reports on the Today programme on 29 May 2003. I shall return to consider this meeting in greater detail at a later stage in this report. After the meeting Mr Gavyn Davies, the Chairman of the BBC issued the following statement:

The BBC Board of Governors met this evening [Sunday 6 July 2003] to discuss the allegations made by Alastair Campbell against the BBC's overall coverage of the Iraq war, and its specific coverage of the September intelligence dossier by Andrew Gilligan in the Today programme.

The Governors questioned Greg Dyke, the Director–General, and Richard Sambrook, the Director of News, about Mr Campbell's allegations. The Board reached the following conclusions.

First, the Board reiterates that the BBC's overall coverage of the war, and the political issues surrounding it, has been entirely impartial, and it emphatically rejects Mr Campbell's claim that large parts of the BBC had an agenda against the war.

We call on Mr Campbell to withdraw these allegations of bias against the BBC and its journalists.

Second, the Board considers that the Today programme properly followed the BBC's Producers' Guidelines in its handling of the Andrew Gilligan report about the September intelligence dossier, which was broadcast on 29 May.

Although the Guidelines say that the BBC should be reluctant to broadcast stories based on a single source, and warn about the dangers of using anonymous sources, they clearly allow for this to be done in exceptional circumstances. Stories based on senior intelligence sources are a case in point.

We note that an entirely separate story was broadcast by an unconnected BBC journalist on Newsnight on 2 June. This story reported very similar allegations to those reported by Andrew Gilligan on the Today programme, but the story has not been singled out for similar criticism by government spokesmen.

Moreover, as these reports fitted in to a general pattern of concern, conveyed to a number of BBC journalists with good contacts in the security services, we consider that it was entirely proper to reflect some unease about the presentation of the Government's arguments in the disputed dossiers.

The Board is satisfied that it was in the public interest to broadcast Mr Gilligan's story, given the information which was available to BBC News at the time. We believe it would not have been in the public interest to have suppressed the stories on either the Today programme or Newsnight.

Third, the Board considers that the Today programme should have kept a clearer account of its dealings with the Ministry of Defence on this story and could have also asked the No 10 Press Office for a response prior to broadcasting the story.

However, we note that firm government denials of the story were broadcast on the Today Programme within 90 minutes of the original broadcast by Andrew Gilligan, and these were followed soon after on the same programme by equally firm denials by a defence minister.

Fourth, the Board intends to look again at the rules under which BBC reporters and presenters are permitted to write for newspapers, once it has received recommendations from the Director of News. This examination will be conducted during the summer.

Finally, the Board wishes to place on record that the BBC has never accused the Prime Minister of lying, or of seeking to take Britain into war under misleading or false pretences.

The BBC did not have an agenda in its war coverage, nor does it now have any agenda which questions the integrity of the Prime Minister.

In summary, the Governors are ultimately responsible for ensuring that the BBC upholds the highest standards of impartiality and accuracy. We are wholly satisfied that BBC journalists and their managers sought to maintain impartiality and accuracy during this episode.

Early on the morning of 7 July between 7 a.m. and 8 a.m. the Prime Minister and Mr Gavyn Davies had a private telephone conversation at the request of the former. The discussion was an amicable one in which each expressed his point of view on the dispute which had arisen between the Government and the BBC but they were unable to reach agreement.

On the morning of Monday 7 July the FAC issued their report on The Decision to go to War in Iraq. At the commencement of their report they set out their Conclusions and Recommendations which included the following:

9. We conclude that the 45 minutes claim did not warrant the prominence given to it in the dossier, because it was based on intelligence from a single, uncorroborated source. We recommend that the Government explain why the claim was given such prominence. (Paragraph 70)

...

11. We conclude that Alastair Campbell did not play any role in the inclusion of the 45 minutes claim in the September dossier. (Paragraph 77)

12. We conclude that it was wrong for Alastair Campbell or any Special Adviser to have chaired a meeting on an intelligence matter, and we recommend that this practice cease. (Paragraph 79)

13. We conclude that on the basis of the evidence available to us Alastair Campbell did not exert or seek to exert improper influence on the drafting of the September dossier. (Paragraph 84)

14. We conclude that the claims made in the September dossier were in all probability well founded on the basis of the intelligence then available, although as we have already stated we have concerns about the emphasis given to some of them. We further conclude that, in the absence of reliable evidence that intelligence personnel have either complained about or sought to distance themselves from the content of the dossier, allegations of politically inspired meddling cannot credibly be established. (Paragraph 86)

15. We conclude that without access to the intelligence or to those who handled it, we cannot know if it was in any respect faulty or misinterpreted. Although without the Foreign Secretary's degree of knowledge, we share his confidence in the men and women who serve in the agencies. (Paragraph 90)

16. We conclude that the language used in the September dossier was in places more assertive than that traditionally used in intelligence documents. We believe that there is much value in retaining the measured and even cautious tones which have been the hallmark of intelligence assessments and we recommend that this approach be retained. (Paragraph 100)

17. We conclude that continuing disquiet and unease about the claims made in the September dossier are unlikely to be dispelled unless more evidence of Iraq's weapons of mass destruction programmes comes to light. (Paragraph 108)

...

26. We recommend that Andrew Gilligan's alleged contacts be thoroughly investigated. We further recommend that the Government review links between the security and intelligence agencies, the media and Parliament and the rules which apply to them. (Paragraph 154) [152].

On the morning of Monday 7 July Mr Scarlett sent the following note to Sir David Omand:

I agree with Kevin Tebbit's letter of Saturday that the finger points strongly at David Kelly as Gilligan's source. I have been through the Gilligan/FAC transcript again. I attach copies of two pages in particular which seem to make it clear that Gilligan has only talked to one person about the September dossier. If he could have referred to any corroborating information he would have done so. If this is true, Kelly is not telling the whole story.

Gilligan must have got the 45 minute single intelligence report item from somewhere, presumably Kelly. Conclusion: Kelly needs a proper security-style interview in which all these inconsistencies are thrashed out. Until we have the full story, we cannot decide what action to take. I think this is rather urgent. Happy to discuss.

Further meetings took place in 10 Downing Street on Monday and Tuesday 7 and 8 July to discuss the course to be followed in the light of Dr Kelly having come forward, and the Prime Minister was present at some of these meetings.

On 21 July 2003 Sir David Omand made a note for the record which was as follows:

### MEETINGS IN THE PRIME MINISTER'S STUDY, 7 AND 8 JULY 2003

7 July

1. I was pulled out of a CMPS [Centre for Management and Policy Studies] lecture at 09.15 on Monday morning, 7 July, with a request to go straight to No.10. I joined a discussion in progress in the PM's study, with the PM, Foreign Secretary, David Manning, Jonathan Powell, Nigel Sheinwald, Sally Morgan. John Scarlett and Kevin Tebbit arrived a little late. Alastair Campbell was also present for part of the meeting.

2. The main subject was discussion of the FAC Report about to issue. There were various advance copies in the room. Lines to take were being prepared. It was noted that the FAC had split largely on party political lines, as the Appendices to the Report showed.

3. There was also a review of the weekend decision not to inform the FAC before the publication of their Report that Dr Kelly had come forward to say that he had met Mr Gilligan. Kevin Tebbit ran over the ground he had covered in his two letters (of Friday 4 and Saturday 5 July). There was some questioning from the PM about what we knew about Dr Kelly, and whether we could find out more about his views. Kevin Tebbit agreed to report back. Kevin Tebbit warned that Dr Kelly was an expert on Iraqi WMD and if he was summoned to give evidence some of it might be uncomfortable on specifics such as the likelihood of there being weapons systems being ready for use within 45 minutes. But he believed from what he had said to Richard Hatfield that Dr Kelly had no doubts that there were Iraqi WMD programmes being concealed from the inspectors. Kevin Tebbit also expressed the view that we would have to face up to the fact that Dr Kelly's name was likely to become public at some point soon, given the number of people he

would have talked to. MOD were preparing contingency statements just in case.

4. There was complete agreement that the inconsistencies in Dr Kelly's story needed to be subject to more forensic examination, and that MOD ought to be considering re-interviewing him. Kevin Tebbit said that MOD were considering calling him back from a conference he was at in order to talk to him again. He reiterated that Dr Kelly had come forward of his volition, and that as far as MOD was concerned there was no question of any offence having been committed under the Official Secrets Act. Dr Kelly's continued co-operation was therefore essential. The Prime Minister made it clear that MOD should continue to handle the case properly, and should follow whatever internal procedures were normal in such cases.

8 July

5. John Scarlett and I were in a videoconference when we were asked to see the PM. I reported orally on further information received from the MOD to the effect that the re-interview had confirmed the earlier story as reported by Kevin Tebbit in his letter on Saturday. It looked as if the main explanation for the Gilligan story of a single source was Dr Kelly, but that Mr Gilligan may well have heavily embellished the conversation, or be drawing on other uncited sources, for the controversial parts of his story.

6. There was discussion (which I may have initiated) of the difficulty that Government witnesses before the ISC would be in if, as was very likely, they were asked whether we had a clue as to the identity of the Gilligan source. I said I would have to reply that we did have someone who had come forward – we could not attempt to cover up this important fact. And I was uneasy that we could be accused of a cover up if we did not tell the FAC, subject to whatever came out of a re-interview. I suggested that we should write to the Chairman of the ISC to tell them that an MOD official had come forward, and thus enable them to inter-

70

view the individual if they thought fit. We could provide the actual name in confidence. The ISC took evidence in private, so confidentiality could be maintained. If we wrote to the FAC (which the FAC might feel was appropriate given that they had just completed a report on the subject) then this could be read as an invitation by them to summon Dr Kelly. We all agreed that the ISC was the proper forum for investigation of this lead, and not the FAC. But the Prime Minister made clear that if, as he suspected, the FAC insisted on calling Dr Kelly to give evidence then we could not in conscience order him not to appear given the relevance of the information he had given us to the FAC's own inquiry. It was accepted at the meeting that copying any ISC letter to the FAC would be tantamount to a public statement, and therefore we should make public in a straightforward way the letter to the ISC. I agreed to write the letter given my position as Security and Intelligence Co-ordinator. MOD would draft with the Cabinet Office. I would make the ISC aware of the actual name of Dr Kelly separately and in confidence.

7. There was also discussion, briefly, of whether the BBC should be informed in advance that a public announcement of an MOD official coming forward was about to be made. We felt there should be, as a courtesy. There was reference to an idea (possibly from MOD) that Mr Hoon should write to either the DG or the Chairman of Governors of the BBC, and after some discussion it was felt that the Chairman was the appropriate person given the Governors' meeting later that evening. It was felt that it would be fair to Dr Kelly to give the BBC the chance to clear his name but it was unreasonable to press the BBC to go further and reveal the name of their source if it was not Dr Kelly. We were clear that they would not do that.

8. Immediately after the meeting at about midday I went to see the Clerk to the ISC, and explain that I was minded to write to the Chairman in those terms. The Clerk expressed some concern, saying that the ISC would not want to be put in a position publicly of having to see an individual; they would make their own mind up on the progress of their

inquiry. He was sure that Ann Taylor would not want to break the Committee rule that they were not giving a public commentary on the progress of their inquiry, and a publication of a letter from me to her might be seen as just that. I then had to leave immediately for Heathrow airport for an official visit to Ottawa. I was informed by telephone that Ann Taylor had confirmed she definitely did not want to receive any letter that was going to be made public. There was confirmation that she however would be prepared to see a reference to the ISC possibly interviewing the individual, if that came at the end of a press statement from Government.

Also on 21 July 2003 Mr John Scarlett made a note which was as follows:

Friday 4 July  Approx 1800: DO [David Omand], DM [David Manning], JSc [John Scarlett], JP [Jonathan Powell]. DO and JSc report from Kevin Tebbit that an MOD official has come forward. Name given. Sounds like Gilligan's source. Noted that normal MOD personnel procedures must be followed and appropriate legal advice taken. Need to think about whether BBC Governors and/or FAC (both of whom deliberate or report in the next three days) should be informed. JP to report to PM [Prime Minister].

Monday 7 July 0900: 10 minute meeting, PM with JP and JSc. Brief discussion of whether Dr K [Dr Kelly] could be the source. PM states that it must be handled according to proper MOD and Civil Service procedures. We need to know more before deciding next steps.

0930: PM meeting with JP, J Straw [Jack Straw], JSc, DO, DM, NS [Nigel Sheinwald], TK [Tom Kelly], AC [Alastair Campbell], SN [Sally Morgan], KT [Kevin Tebbit]. Main purpose to discuss FAC report. Brief discussion of MOD source. If he appeared before a Committee, would he be likely to support or otherwise the Government position? JSc to seek advice from MOD. Was he or was he not the source? No further decision possible without knowing more about his contact with Gilligan.

KT asked to arrange a further interview as soon as possible. On leaving meeting KT to issue instructions for Dr K to come to London for interview.

Tuesday 8 July 0815: PM internal meeting to prepare for Liaison Committee. JP, AC, JSc, CS [Claire Sumner], CR [Catherine Rimmer], J Straw, DM, MR [Matthew Rycroft], TK (not all at once as I recall). At end PM wonders what to say if LC [Liaison Committee] asked about leak inquiries. Does PM have any idea about source? PM anxious not to be misleading if some kind of statement likely later in the day or next day. Eventually conclude that he must not trail a possible statement about anyone coming forward. He would reply, if asked, that we were taking the possibility of leaks seriously and looking at this in the normal way.

Circa 1145: PM meeting. DO, JSc, DM, JP, AC. Discussed informing ISC. SDO to send letter, JSc to draft. Do not want to involve FAC but if name becoming public they would be bound to ask to interview him. Agreement that the issue would inevitably become public. We were already open to criticism for not coming clean about the existence of a possible source. Not much time left. Also discussion of a letter from GH [Geoff Hoon] to Chairman BBC Governors.

1330: PM meeting. JP, JSc, AC, TK. Discussed draft letter to ISC. Word received from Ann Taylor that she does not want to receive it. Do press statement instead. Decide to draft press statement with separate private letter from GH to BBC Chairman giving the name. Discussion of how BBC will react (will they be ready to discuss this in businesslike way). If Dr K name becomes public will Government be criticised for putting him under 'wider pressure'? PM repeats that MOD must remain in charge and follow their procedures.

At a meeting in 10 Downing Street on 7 July at which the Prime Minister and the Foreign Secretary, Mr Jack Straw MP, were present it was decided that Dr

Kelly should be further interviewed to find out more about what he had said to Mr Gilligan. Mr Dominic Wilson, the Private Secretary to Sir Kevin Tebbit sent Mr Hatfield the following minute which was also sent to Mr Martin Howard and Dr Wells. The minute was dated 8 July but it was drafted by Mr Wilson on 7 July and was read over to Mr Hatfield before the interview with Dr Kelly on that day. The minute was as follows:

GILLIGAN: INTERVIEW WITH DR KELLY
PUS was grateful for your minute of 7 July and record of your discussions with Dr Kelly.

2. What is now needed is a more intensive interview with Kelly. The objective would be to establish what transpired between him and Gilligan, with a reliability that will stand up to the intense glare of public scrutiny. The core issue in this respect is whether it was Kelly who alleged that the 45 minute intelligence was inserted into the dossier against the wishes of the intelligence community and at the behest of the Government in general and Alastair Campbell in particular.

3. PUS believes that this must be pinned down as clearly as possible because of the continuing problem with the BBC and the FAC's recommendation that Gilligan's contacts should be investigated. It should also be in Kelly's own interest for this to occur, given that at least one of his colleagues has already speculated that he could indeed be Gilligan's 'single anonymous source' and Kelly's own view (as we understand it) that this would be a misrepresentation of the position.

4. Against this background I understand that arrangements have been made for the further interview to be carried out by you and addresses (sic) at 1600 today. The PUS would like to consider in the light of this whether to recommend a public announcement. The key issues will be:

a. a judgment of the probability that Kelly is in (sic) the principal source of Gilligan's allegations – wittingly or otherwise (and the credibility of alternative explanations);

b. Kelly's readiness to be associated with a public statement that names him and carries a clear and sustainable refutation of the core allegation on the '45 minute' intelligence;

c. our view about the robustness of the rest of his position, including on Iraq's WMD programmes generally.

5. In all this PUS remains concerned to ensure that Dr Kelly's rights are respected – it is important that he understands he is cooperating voluntarily. There is also the different angle that in the event that it becomes evident that he may have divulged classified or privileged information contrary to the position so far, proceedings would need to be stopped immediately to avoid prejudicing any case that might then need to be brought.

On Monday 7 July Mr Alastair Campbell issued the following press statement:

I am very pleased that the FAC (Foreign Affairs Select Committee) inquiry has found that the allegations made against me broadcast by the BBC are untrue.

These allegations were that I was responsible for the insertion of the 45-minute intelligence into the WMD (weapons of mass destruction) dossier, against the wishes of the Intelligence Agencies, whilst probably knowing it to be wrong.

This was then repeated over five weeks. These allegations are all false as the FAC has found. Indeed, even Sir John Stanley has said on this, the BBC was wrong.

I want to make it clear yet again that I fully respect the independence of the BBC.

There can be a dispute between us as to whether they should ever have run the original story.

But surely there can be no dispute that the allegations, whether or not sources, are untrue.

Even now, all that I ask is that the BBC accept this, and I note that at no point did the BBC Governors in their statement last night claim that the story was true, merely that the BBC were within their rights to run it. This issue – the truth of the claims – is the only issue, and the one that the BBC should be addressing.

I am saddened that, for whatever reason and despite overwhelming evidence, they still refuse to admit that the allegations they broadcast were false.

On 7 July the BBC also issued the following press statement:

The BBC believes today's report from the Foreign Affairs Committee justifies its decision to broadcast the Today programme story of 29 May and the Newsnight story of 2 June and shows that both were in the public interest.

In particular, we believe the decision to highlight the circumstances surrounding the 45 minute claim has been vindicated.

We would point to the unanimous conclusion of the Foreign Affairs Committee in paragraphs 70 and 71, which says:

'We conclude that the 45 minute claim did not warrant the prominence given to it in the dossier, because it was based on intelligence based on a single uncorroborated source. We recommend that the Government explain why the claim was given such prominence.'

The committee continues: 'We further recommend that in its response to this report, the Government set out whether it still considers the September dossier to be accurate in what it states about the 45 minute claim, in the light of subsequent events.'

It is because of BBC journalism that the problems surrounding the 45 minute claim have come to light and been given proper public attention.

We note that the committee was deeply divided on the role Alastair Campbell played in the compilation of the September dossier and only reached a decision which supported his position on the casting vote of the Labour chairman. We also note that not all the Labour MPs on the committee supported this decision.

We also consider it important, in the context of our reporting, that in paragraph 100 the committee says unanimously:

'The language used in the September dossier was more assertive than that traditionally used in intelligence documents.'

And in paragraph 107, the committee says: 'We conclude that the continuing disquiet and unease about the claims made in the September dossier are unlikely to be dispelled unless more evidence of Iraq's WMD programmes come to light.'

We are pleased that Alastair Campbell said this morning that his complaint is about one story only and was no longer an attack on the whole of the BBC's journalism or coverage of the war.

On whether or not it was right for the BBC to broadcast the Today programme story on 29 May, the BBC will have to agree to disagree with Mr Campbell. The Foreign Affairs Select Committee makes no comment on this.

On Monday 7 July Dr Kelly was attending a course of pre-deployment training at the RAF station at Honington in Suffolk prior to leaving for Baghdad later that week. Dr Kelly was asked to return to London to be interviewed and he was interviewed on the afternoon of 7 July by Mr Hatfield and Mr Howard in the presence of Dr Wells. On 8 July Mr Hatfield wrote to Sir Kevin Tebbit as follows:

1. I saw Dr Kelly again yesterday afternoon in company with Martin Howard and Bryan Wells.

2. As I told you last night, there was no change in the essentials of his story and in particular he stoutly maintains that, as in his original letter, he did not make accusations about the dossier and, in particular, did not suggest that any material had been added by Downing Street. Some of his other replies suggested that he had become rather more concerned that some of his background comments might have been regarded by

Gilligan as providing collateral for his thesis and may well have been incorporated with information from other sources. As Kelly himself put it, 'I am beginning to realise that I might have been led on!'

3. I made it clear to Dr Kelly that, given the FAC outcome and particularly the recommendation to try to follow up Gilligan's contacts, it was likely that the MOD would have to reveal that someone had come forward to admit talking to Gilligan. I said that I did not think that it would be necessary to reveal his name or to go into detail beyond indicating that the account given to us did not match Gilligan's PAC account, at least initially. It was, however, quite likely that his name would come out, not least because speculation about the nature of the source (eg the Times of 5 July 2003) might lead in his direction. It was also possible that, depending on further developments, the FAC might seek to call him as a witness. It was therefore very important that he should tell us if there was anything that he had omitted or was unsure about. Dr Kelly confirmed that there was nothing that he wanted to change or add. He also agreed that the attached draft press statement accurately reflected his position and that he would stand by it if questioned. I gave him a copy and said that we would try to give him advance warning of any announcement but circumstances might make this impossible. (I re–confirmed this understanding on the telephone this morning, when agreeing that he could complete his training at RAF Honington today).

4. I also attach a slightly updated version of my comparative analysis which reflects clarifications to some of the detail as a result of the second interview with Kelly. I have also tidied up serials 2 and 3, where my original comment was slightly misleading. Kelly first remembers speaking to Gilligan at the IISS seminar in September 2002 in a coffee break but his two arranged meetings with Gilligan were both this year, in February and May, before and after Gilligan's trip to Iraq. On reflection, the discrepancy with Gilligan's evidence to the FAC that he had not seen his contact face to face for 'about a year' is even greater. If the contact is Kelly this would mean that Gilligan was overlooking the meeting this

February, as well as referring to a meeting which appears to have taken place in May 2002 before Kelly had met him.

The draft press statement attached to Mr Hatfield's letter of 8 July was as follows:

An individual working in the MOD has volunteered that he met with Andrew Gilligan on 22 May to discuss Gilligan's experiences as a correspondent in Iraq. This was one week before Gilligan's story claiming that the September 2002 Iraq dossier had been 'sexed up'. The account of the meeting given by this official does not match the account given by Gilligan to the Foreign Affairs Committee of his 'single source'. The official has told up that he made no allegations or accusations about the dossier and, in particular, did not suggest that any material had been added to the dossier by Alastair Campbell or Downing Street against the wishes of the intelligence community. He is not a member of the Intelligence Services or the Defence Intelligence Staff.

This discussion was not authorised in accordance with departmental guidance for contact with the media. This is being dealt with appropriately by line management.

There is no reason to suspect that a breach of security is involved.

Dr Wells made the following note of the meeting:

Present:
Mr Martin Howard, DCDI
Mr Richard Hatfield, Personnel Director
Dr Bryan Wells, DCPAC
Dr David Kelly, CPAC Special Adviser

1. Hatfield started by saying that he wanted the meeting to cover two issues. The first was to follow up the discrepancies between Gilligan's account of the meeting with his source, and Kelly's account of his meeting with Gilligan. The second issue was that MOD may wish to make a

public statement, and he wished to discuss that with Kelly. The meeting was structured to follow Hatfield's comparative analysis circulated under his minute of 8 July to PS/PUS.

2. Serials 2 and 3. Hatfield said that Kelly had described the IISS Seminar in September 2002 as being the first time that he had consciously met Gilligan. Hatfield probed whether Kelly had indeed never met Gilligan before. Kelly replied that he could not recall having spoken to Gilligan before then. They certainly had not had a meeting or a purposeful discussion. Hatfield probed further; surely Kelly could not have forgotten such a meeting. Kelly replied that he could not recall one.

3. Hatfield then asked about the meeting between Kelly and Gilligan in February 2003. Kelly replied that the meeting was held at the Charing Cross Hotel and lasted for 45 minutes to 1 hour. It had taken place at Gilligan's suggestion. He could not recall having had any further contact until May.

4. Howard asked whether Kelly talked to journalists a lot. Kelly replied that he would have people contact him 3–4 times a week. Many of the calls were quite simply asking technical details. Howard commented that a non–technical discussion with Gilligan would therefore have stuck out.

5. Serials 4 and 5. Hatfield asked Kelly to describe in detail his involvement in the government's dossier of September 2002. Kelly said that to his recollection the idea of a dossier arose in April 2002. He had drafted his contributions (described in his letter of 30 June) during May and June 2002. He then recalled that the subject went into limbo. He was on leave for two weeks in August and then on duty in New York and consequently was not involved in any work during that month. His only subsequent involvement was when he was asked by DIS (in September) to look at the passages on biological weapons and consider whether anything extra could be added. He had suggested including a discussion

of Smallpox, but that was subsequently rejected on the grounds of there being inadequate intelligence. That was the sum of his involvement. Howard asked if he had [been] contacted in order to check textual amendments. Kelly replied that he had not. Howard also asked if Kelly had discussed the dossier with DIS staff. Kelly replied that he could not recall any in depth discussion. He recalled that there had not in any case been much discussion of the dossier at the time. He reminded the meeting that he had never acknowledged outside Government that he had contributed to the dossier.

6. Serial 6. Hatfield asked how Kelly described himself to Gilligan. Kelly replied that he assumed Gilligan would know that he was a senior adviser to DPACS/DCPAC. People had all sorts of ideas about his role; he continued to have a high profile on UNSCOM/UNMOVIC work; and a number of people believe that he was an intelligence officer. Hatfield asked if Gilligan thought that he was part of the intelligence agencies. Kelly replied that he could not exclude that possibility although he would not describe himself as such and would not have encouraged Gilligan to think it.

7. Serial 10. Howard asked if Gilligan had taken notes of the meeting. Kelly replied that Gilligan had produced a small notebook and pencil and had taken some notes but these were not copious.

8. Serial 8. Hatfield recalled that Kelly had been clear that the May meeting with Gilligan lasted 45 minutes. He asked the basis for this. Kelly replied that the meeting had been fixed for 17.00 hours. He clearly recalled Gilligan turning up at 17.15. He believed that he left at about 18.00 to catch the 18.30 Paddington train.

9. Serial 11. Hatfield referred to the quotation from Gilligan's source that the dossier was 'transformed the week before it was published to make it sexier'. He asked Kelly if he had said this or something similar. Kelly said that he had not described the dossier as having been trans-

formed the week before publication, and could not recall using the term 'sexier'. Hatfield probed: had Kelly said anything that could be construed as being that quotation? Kelly said that he could not recall; his memory was that discussion of the dossier was fleeting. Hatfield commented that the flavour of Gilligan's evidence to the FAC was that the meeting concentrated on the dossier: that was why the differing accounts of the meeting's length were important: a longer meeting would have allowed more discussion of the issues. Howard referred to the passage in Kelly's letter of 30 June where he said that the '45 minutes claim' was included in the dossier for 'impact'. Was this the exact word used or was it a paraphrase? Kelly replied that he would use that word on occasion, but could not recall if he had said it to Gilligan. But he would not use the phrase to imply criticism: he meant it in the sense that the claim was in the forward (sic) signed by the Prime Minister, rather than simply in the body of the text. It therefore had 'impact' in that sense.

10. Serial 13. Howard asked if Kelly had seen the intelligence report relating to the '45 minutes claim'. Kelly replied that he had not. Howard asked if Kelly was aware that there was intelligence on the subject. Kelly replied that he was not, until the issue was in the public domain. Hatfield referred to the quote from Gilligan's source which said that 'WMD were ready for use in 45 minutes ... not in original draft ... included against their wishes because it wasn't reliable'. Did Kelly say this? Kelly replied that he could not believe that he would have said this: he did not say that it was not in the original draft; and he didn't know the wishes of the intelligence services. Hatfield asked what question Gilligan was asking Kelly to respond to when the '45 minute claim' came up. Kelly replied that they were discussing why WMD had not been used during the conflict. He had explained his own view which was that weather conditions had prevented use early in the campaign, and breakdown of C2 had prevented its use in the later commented (sic) that this was different from Gilligan's description to the FAC. Kelly continued that he wondered now if he had been led on by Gilligan. His stock answer on

the '45 minutes claim' that was in the early 90s, Iraq had a policy to fill to use. But this still required transportation of the stored armaments to launch sites for their use. All this was time–consuming. He therefore could not relate the claim to anything he knew of. But he recognised that he was not familiar with all the systems.

11. Serial 14. Hatfield asked Kelly about his discussions on uranium imports from Niger. Kelly said that so far as he could recall it was not discussed in depth. He would not have said anything other than to note the IAEA observations on the issue.

12. Serial 16. Hatfield asked if Kelly had discussed with Gilligan the role of Alastair Campbell in the dossier. Kelly replied that, as he had said in his letter of 30 June, Gilligan did raise the involvement of Campbell and Kelly said that he was unable to comment. Hatfield asked in what context the role of Alastair Campbell had been raised. Kelly replied that it was in the context of the editing process of the dossier. Hatfield asked what Kelly meant by being 'unable to comment'. Kelly replied that it would have been a dismissive response. Hatfield asked specifically if Kelly had himself referred to 'Campbell'. Kelly replied that he had not.

13. Serial 17. Hatfield asked if Kelly had said that Downing Street 'had asked repeatedly if anything could be added to the original draft'. Kelly replied that he had not.

14. Serial 18. Hatfield asked if there had been any discussion of the Iraqi source for the '45 minutes claim'. Kelly replied that he had no idea who the source was and did not speculate on that source with Gilligan. Hatfield asked Kelly if he had told Gilligan that Iraq had not been able to weaponise CBW. Kelly replied that he had not said this and he believed otherwise.

15. Serial 24. Hatfield asked Kelly if he would have said whether (sic) that there was a 30% probability of there being a CW programme in the

six months before the war. Kelly replied that 30% was the sort of figure he would use as the probability for there having been a current production programme. He was 100% certain that there had been a chemical weapon programme.

16. Serial 25. Hatfield asked if Kelly had said or believed that the Iraqi WMD threat was smaller and less imminent than that claimed by the government. Kelly replied that he believed the threat was both current and specific.

17. Howard asked if Kelly was aware of anyone else who could have been a source for Gilligan. Kelly replied that he was not aware of any sources. He was aware that some points of his description of the meeting with Gilligan matched those of Gilligan's description of his meeting with the source. Kelly said that he was concerned that Gilligan would try to hang the other stories on to him.

18. Howard asked if anybody from the BBC, and in particular Gilligan, had tried to contact Kelly since the meeting on May 22. Kelly replied that Gilligan had not tried to contact him. The only BBC person he could recall having contacted him was Susan Watts, a science editor.

19. Hatfield said that it was likely that the department would need to make some public statement on Kelly's involvement with Gilligan. He passed Kelly a draft press release and Kelly confirmed that he was content with its terms. Hatfield said that although Kelly was not named in the press release his identity may become known in due course. Kelly replied that he acknowledged this: in his letter of 30 June he had said that a friend at RUSI had alerted him to the possibility of his being considered as Gilligan's source.

On 8 July Mr Hoon had a lunchtime meeting with Mr Richard Sambrook, the Director of News at the BBC, to discuss the MoD's concern that Mr Gilligan had not forewarned it of the WMD allegations which he broadcast on 29 May.

At a meeting in 10 Downing Street on Tuesday 8 July commencing at 1.30pm it was learnt that Mrs Ann Taylor MP, the Chairman of the ISC did not want to receive a letter informing her that the civil servant had come forward (see Mr Scarlett's note set out in paragraph 61). It was then decided to issue a press statement that a civil servant working in the MoD had come forward to say that he had met Mr Gilligan on 22 May. A group of officials comprising Sir Kevin Tebbit, Mr John Scarlett, Mr Jonathan Powell, Mr Alastair Campbell and Mr Tom Kelly then began to draft the statement in 10 Downing Street.

During the first part of the afternoon of 8 July Dr Kelly was at RAF Honington and just after 3.30pm Mr Hatfield was telephoned by Mr Wilson, the Private Secretary to Sir Kevin Tebbit, who told him that it was expected that the MoD would need to make a statement about Dr Kelly that evening and that he (Mr Hatfield) was going to be asked to clear the text with Dr Kelly when it was available. At that point the text had not been sent to Mr Hatfield but Mr Wilson read the text over to him. Mr Hatfield then rang Dr Kelly hoping to speak to him before he left RAF Honington but he got Dr Kelly's mobile telephone voicemail and left him a message saying that he wanted to talk to him as soon as possible about the possible release of a statement and about the text of that statement. Dr Kelly called Mr Hatfield back at 4.14pm and Mr Hatfield repeated the message which he had previously left on his voicemail. Mr Hatfield also told Dr Kelly that the statement was likely to be slightly longer than the one which they had discussed on the previous day because the text was going to say a little more about what Dr Kelly had told the MoD officials he had said to Mr Gilligan. Mr Hatfield still did not have the text of the statement which was to be issued and he said to Dr Kelly that they would need to talk again in half an hour or so. Soon after that telephone conversation Mr Hatfield received the text of the press statement. Mr Hatfield telephoned Dr Kelly again at 5.10pm and read through the statement to him paragraph by paragraph and when Mr Hatfield had finished reading the text Dr Kelly said that he was content with it. Mr Hatfield told Dr Kelly that the statement would be issued very soon and that he was certain it would be out by 7.00pm. Mr Hatfield also told him in that conversation or in the earlier telephone conversation at 4.14pm that he should talk to the press office and to Dr Wells about support.

The press statement was issued by the MoD about 5.45pm on Tuesday 8

July in the following terms:

An individual working in the MOD has come forward to volunteer that he met Andrew Gilligan of the BBC on May 22. It was an unauthorised meeting. It took place one week before Mr Gilligan broadcast allegations against the Government about the WMD dossier on the Today programme.

The person who has come forward has volunteered that he has known Mr Gilligan for some months. He says that he met Mr Gilligan in a central London hotel at Mr Gilligan's request. During the conversation Mr Gilligan raised the Iraqi WMD programme, including the '45 minutes' issue. The official says that Mr Gilligan also raised the issue of Alastair Campbell.

The individual is an expert on WMD who has advised ministers on WMD and whose contribution to the Dossier of September 2002 was to contribute towards drafts of historical accounts of UN inspections. He is not 'one of the senior officials in charge of drawing up the dossier'. He is not a member of the Intelligence Services or the Defence Intelligence Staff.

He says that when Mr Gilligan asked about the role of Alastair Campbell with regard to the 45 minute issue, he made no comment and explained that he was not involved in the process of drawing up the intelligence parts of the Dossier.

He says he made no other comment about Mr Campbell. When Mr Gilligan asked him why the 45 minute point was in the Dossier, he says he commented that it was 'probably for impact'. He says he did not see the 45 minute intelligence report on which it was based.

He has said that, as an expert in the field, he believes Saddam Hussein possessed WMD.

We do not know whether this official is the single source quoted by Mr Gilligan. Mr Gilligan told the FAC he had only one source for his story, and that the other three sources he mentioned to the FAC did not talk to him about the September Dossier, or did so after the broadcast.

The MOD, with the individual's agreement, intend to give his name to the Chairman of the Intelligence and Security Committee, in confidence, should they wish to interview him as part of their inquiry.

On the evening of Tuesday 8 July, after the press statement had been issued, Ms Pamela Teare, the Director of News in the MoD, and Mrs Kate Wilson, the chief press officer in the MoD, had a discussion and agreed that the latter should telephone Dr Kelly to alert him to the high level of media interest in the statement and to advise him that he might want to consider staying with friends. Accordingly, Mrs Wilson telephoned Dr Kelly on his mobile. She called him at 8.26pm when he said he was out walking and asked her to call him back. She then called Dr Kelly back about twenty minutes later and told him that the statement had been put out. She wanted to make sure that he had her contact numbers but he said that he did not have anything to write with and so he could not take her numbers down. Mrs Wilson then asked him if he had the number for the duty press officer and he said he did. Mrs Wilson told him that the MoD press office had had a lot of follow up questions and that he needed to think about alternative accommodation. She did not offer him accommodation because her view was that it was better to go and stay with family or friends than to go to a hotel, and that is what she recommended to him. She asked him if there was anything he wanted from her and he said there was not. Mrs Wilson said in evidence that it was a brief conversation. When asked how Dr Kelly sounded at the time she replied that he was not surprised by anything she said and he seemed very calm.

On 8 July Mr Hoon wrote to Mr Gavyn Davies, the Chairman of the Board of Governors of the BBC, enclosing the MoD's statement and saying:

> I am writing to draw to your attention an MOD statement which we shall be issuing later today about Andrew Gilligan's 'single source'. This is enclosed.
>
> You will see that we have not named the official within the MOD who has come forward. We would, however, be prepared to disclose his name to you in confidence, on the basis that you would then immediately confirm or deny that this is indeed Mr Gilligan's source, in the

interests of resolving what has become a management problem for both our organisations.

I am sure you will understand that this is not the same as divulging a source since the individual has come forward.

Mr Gavyn Davies replied to Mr Hoon on the 8 July and stated:

Thank you for today's letter, which I believe you have now released to the press.

I have to say that the offer in your letter seems to be an attempt to force the BBC News Division to reveal the name or names of the source(s) used by Andrew Gilligan on Today and Susan Watts on Newsnight. You will recognise that it is a cardinal principle of good journalism that sources should never be revealed, no matter how intense the pressure may be. As Chairman of the BBC, I support this principle.

In line with this principle, I do not myself know the identity [of] the source(s) mentioned above, so I am unable to accept your offer of confirming whether their name(s) match the person who has come forward at the Ministry of Defence.

I will be releasing this letter to the press.

On the evening of 8 July the BBC issued a press statement:

We note that today, the Ministry of Defence has issued a statement saying that an individual working in the Ministry of Defence has come forward to volunteer information about an unauthorised meeting he says he had with Andrew Gilligan on May 22.

The description of the individual contained in the statement does not match Mr Gilligan's source in some important ways.

Mr Gilligan's source does not work in the Ministry of Defence and he has known the source for a number of years not months.

As we have said before, Mr Gilligan met several people in the period before the story was broadcast and discussed Weapons of Mass Destruction in various ways with a number of them.

His Today programme story was based on only one of those conversations.

For the single conversation which led to the Today story, Mr Gilligan took comprehensive notes during the meeting with his source which do not correspond with the account given in the MoD statement.

These notes have already been deposited with the BBC legal department.

We note that the MoD statement says that 'we do not know whether this official is Mr Gilligan's source'.

Neither do we.

What we do know is that Mr Gilligan's notes and account of what he was told are very similar to the notes of a conversation Susan Watts, Science Editor of Newsnight, had with her source which led to the Newsnight reports of June 2 and 4.

These reports contained allegations consistent with the Gilligan report and she described her source as 'a senior official intimately involved with [the] process of pulling together the September dossier'.

We reiterate the point we made last week that Susan Watts and Andrew Gilligan have never met, spoken or corresponded about any issues let alone this particular matter.

We do not know whether their respective sources are the same person, as Susan Watts and George Entwhistle, the Editor of Newsnight, are unwilling to reveal her source.

However, if it is the same source, it is quite clear that the information he is now giving to the Ministry of Defence is not a full and frank account of the conversation with Mr Gilligan and that he has failed to mention the conversation with Susan Watts.

If it is a different source, it means that the original Gilligan story was separately corroborated by a second source – the person who spoke to Susan Watts.

Either way, we stand by Mr Gilligan's reporting of his source.

On 9 July Mr Hoon wrote to Mr Davies and stated:

Thank you for your letter of 8 July replying to mine of the same day.

This is not about the divulging of sources.

So that you can establish whether the name of the person who has come forward is the same as the name given to BBC Management by Andrew Gilligan, I am now prepared to tell you that his name is David Kelly, advisor to the Proliferation and Arms Control Secretariat in the MOD.

I trust that the BBC Internal Inquiry into Mr Gilligan's dealings with the MOD Press Office will be broadened to include this matter.

Mr Davies' office was informed by the MoD that it would not be releasing this letter to the press.

On 10 July Mr Davies replied to Mr Hoon stating:

Thank you for your letter of 9th July. I have discussed the matter with Greg Dyke as Editor-in-Chief. Although I did not originally show him the name contained in your letter, I am sure he will have now seen the name in most of this morning's newspapers.

The BBC will not be making any more comments about, or responding to any claims concerning, the identity of Andrew Gilligan's source for his story on the Today programme on May 29, or the identity of Susan Watts' source for her story on Newsnight on 2nd June.

On the afternoon of Friday 4 July Ms Pamela Teare, the Director of News in the MoD and Mrs Wilson, the Chief Press Officer in the MoD, prepared contingent briefings which might be used by MoD press officers in the form of Questions and Answers in case the press became aware in some way over the weekend that a civil servant had come forward to say that he had met Mr Gilligan on 22 May. In the course of the next few days until Tuesday 8 July these Questions and Answers were revised by Ms Teare and Mrs Wilson a number of times but they were not given to senior officials for their approval. On 8 July Ms Teare and Mr Martin Howard did further work on the Q and A material and after the decision had been taken to issue a press statement that an unnamed civil servant had come forward it was decided by the MoD that if the press put the correct name, ie Dr Kelly's name, to a government press officer the press officer would confirm it. The first draft of the Question and Answer material contained the following sentences:

> Who is the official?

> We are not prepared to name the individual involved.

> Why not?

> We have released all the relevant details. There is nothing to gain by revealing the name of the individual who has come forward voluntarily.

The final form of the Question and Answer material contained the following sentence:

> If the correct name is given, we can confirm it and say that he is senior advisor to the Proliferation and Arms Control Secretariat.

After the MoD had issued the press statement in the late afternoon of 8 July the MoD press office was inundated with calls seeking more information but no member of the press suggested Dr Kelly's name.

On Wednesday 9 July there continued to be a great volume of press interest in the name of the civil servant who had come forward and the MoD press office received many calls from the media seeking more information and trying to identify the civil servant. Press officers in the MoD used the Question and Answer material which had been given to them and did not volunteer Dr Kelly's name. In the late afternoon, about 5.30pm, the *Financial Times* put Dr Kelly's name to Ms Teare who confirmed it. Shortly afterwards, the *Guardian*, the *Daily Mail* and the *Daily Telegraph* put Dr Kelly's name to a press officer and the name was confirmed. The *Times* put twenty names until Dr Kelly's name was put and confirmed.

About 6.00pm on 9 July Mrs Wilson heard that Dr Kelly's name had been confirmed to the press. She then telephoned Sir Kevin Tebbit's office about 6.15pm and requested his Private Secretary, Mr Wilson, to ask Dr Wells to ring Dr Kelly to tell him that his name had been confirmed to the press. It appears that Mr Wilson tried to contact Dr Wells by telephone for about half an hour and finally got in touch with him about 7.00pm when Dr Wells was on a train travelling home. Mr Wilson passed on to him the message from Mrs Wilson requesting him to tell Dr Kelly that the press office had confirmed his name to the press. Dr Wells then rang Dr Kelly at 7.03pm from the train on his mobile telephone and told him that he had been asked to pass on the message that the press office had confirmed his name to the press and Dr Wells advised him to get in touch with the press office. This call lasted for 46 seconds, it was a bad line and Dr Wells thought that they were cut off. Dr Kelly rang Dr Wells back at 7.09pm when Dr Wells was still on his train. Dr Wells thought that Dr Kelly had called him back because the earlier telephone call had been cut off and he repeated to Dr Kelly that the press office had confirmed his name.

In the late afternoon of 9 July Mr Nicholas Rufford, a reporter from the Sunday Times, who had met Dr Kelly at his home on previous occasions to discuss his work, drove to Dr Kelly's house in Oxfordshire because he suspected that Dr Kelly might be the person who had spoken to Mr Gilligan. He arrived at Dr Kelly's house about 7.30pm and saw him in the garden. The first words which Dr Kelly spoke to him were that he had just had a call from the MoD telling him that he would be named in national newspapers the following day. Mr Rufford told him that the press were on their way in droves and offered to provide him with hotel accommodation on behalf of his newspaper. Mr Rufford had some further conversation with Dr Kelly and left his garden about 7.45pm.

At 7.54pm when Dr Wells had got off his train and when communication was clearer between the two of them, Dr Wells called Dr Kelly again on his mobile telephone to check that he had got his earlier message and that he was acting on it and Dr Kelly told him that Nick Rufford had appeared on his doorstep.

After having spoken to Mr Wilson about 6.30pm, Mrs Wilson took steps to arrange that a press officer would be ready to go to Dr Kelly's house if Dr Kelly wanted him. She was about to telephone Dr Kelly about 8.00pm when Dr

Kelly telephoned her and said that Nick Rufford had been in contact with him and asked him why he was not now in a hotel. Dr Kelly told Mrs Wilson that he was now minded to go to family or friends and he would be heading to the West Country, but he would let her know where he was when he got there.

Dr Kelly and his wife then packed some clothes very quickly and left their house in a rush within ten minutes. They drove towards Weston-Super-Mare and on the way they stopped just outside Swindon about 8.45pm and Dr Kelly telephoned Dr Wells and told him that he was travelling to Cornwall. Dr and Mrs Kelly spent the night of 9 July in Weston-Super-Mare. On the morning of Thursday 10 July Dr Kelly telephoned Dr Wells and they agreed to keep in touch.

# Chapter Four

On 10 July Mr Donald Anderson MP, the Chairman of the FAC, wrote to Mr Hoon stating:

> The Foreign Affairs Committee wishes to receive an answer to the following question.
>
> On what date, and at what time, did the meeting take place between Dr David Kelly and Mr Andrew Gilligan at which the conversation referred to in the MoD statement of 9 July (sic) took place?
>
> You will wish to know that the Clerk is writing to Dr Kelly today, inviting him, to appear before the Committee to give oral evidence in public on Tuesday 15 July, on questions directly relevant to the Committee's Report published earlier this week, arising from the MoD statement of 9 July (sic).

On 10 July the Clerk of the FAC wrote to Dr Kelly stating:

> The Foreign Affairs Committee wishes to hear oral evidence from you in public at 3 o'clock on Tuesday 15 July, to answer questions directly relevant to the Committee's Report published earlier this week, arising from the MoD statement of 9 July (sic).

On 10 July the Clerk of the ISC made an oral request to the MoD that Dr Kelly should give evidence before that Committee on 15 July.

On 10 July Sir Kevin Tebbit wrote to Mr Hoon stating:

There have been requests to you for Dr Kelly to appear before both the FAC and the ISC (on the same day, 15 July).

2. We had already offered him to the ISC and I recommend that you agree to that request, although to avoid setting a precedent, you should stress that you only are content for such a relatively junior official to appear given the exceptional nature of the evidence that Dr Kelly could offer. As regards the FAC, however, I recommend that you resist, on grounds that the FAC inquiry is completed (their report was finalised on 3 July, before we had been able to talk to Kelly ourselves) and that a separate session to question Kelly would attach disproportionate importance to him in relation to the subject of their inquiry as a whole. The ISC, on the other hand, are only just beginning their work and are better placed to ensure that Kelly's views are placed in the proper context (he is, after all, not the Government's principal adviser on the subject, nor even a senior one). A further benefit of an ISC hearing is that they can more easily handle national security dimensions, should they wish to cover intelligence material with Kelly, although they might be prepared, given the public interest, to hold most of their hearing in open session, although this could be unprecedented.

3. A further reason for avoiding two hearings, back to back, is to show some regard for the man himself. He has come forward voluntarily, is not used to being thrust into the public eye, and is not on trial. It does not seem unreasonable to ask the FAC to show restraint and accept the FAC hearing as being sufficient for their purposes (eg testing the validity of Gilligan's evidence).

4. It will, of course, be important to ensure that views that Kelly may express are not necessarily taken to represent HMG's policy, or even the collective view of either our intelligence or military expert communities. The ISC will be suitably placed to deal with this through the further witnesses they already plan to call, eg John Scarlett. The FAC, with their hearing ended and report produced, would not be in that position.

5. This line may not be sustainable in strict institutional terms: the FAC report to Parliament, whereas the ISC, although drawn from Parliament, report formally to the Prime Minister. And I do not believe that the ISC have taken testimony in public before.

But I think it worth a try at least. The individual himself is, I understand, prepared to appear before both bodies.

On Friday 11 July Mr Hoon's Private Secretary wrote to Mr Straw's Private Secretary as follows:

As you know, the Defence Secretary received a letter yesterday afternoon from the Chairman of the Foreign Affairs Committee, Donald Anderson, asking that Dr David Kelly should appear before the FAC on Tuesday 15 July at 1500. At about the same time, we received an oral request from the Clerk to the Intelligence and Security Committee (ISC) asking for Dr Kelly to appear before them on the same day at 1230 for about 45 minutes. Donald Anderson has asked for a reply by 1600 today. The Government has already indicated, in the MOD press statement issued on Tuesday 8 July, that it would not object if the ISC asked to see Dr Kelly as part of their current inquiry.

The Defence Secretary has given the request from the FAC careful consideration. There are reasons for resisting this request:

The FAC have already completed their inquiry. (Indeed, their report was finalised on 3 July before MOD officials had interviewed Dr Kelly themselves.)

A separate session to question Dr Kelly would attach disproportionate importance to him in relation to the subject of the FAC's inquiry as a whole.

The ISC is better placed than the FAC to handle the national security dimensions should the question of intelligence material arise.

It is fairer on the man himself not to expect him to appear before two Parliamentary Committees within the space of 3 hours.

On the other hand:

It is not unreasonable for the FAC to feel that Dr Kelly's account may call into question the evidence that they were given by Andrew Gilligan and that they should therefore have an opportunity to see him themselves. (It is conceivable, that having done so, they may decide to recall Gilligan.)

Presentationally, it would be difficult to defend a position in which the Government had objected to Dr Kelly appearing before a Committee of the House which takes evidence in public in favour of an appointed Committee which meets in private. Although the ISC has considered taking evidence in public before and might decide to do so on this occasion, this could set an unwelcome precedent for both the Committee itself and for us.

The Defence Secretary has, therefore, concluded that on balance we should agree to the FAC's request. Given that Dr Kelly is a relatively junior official who played only a limited role in the preparation of the Dossier, we should invite Donald Anderson to agree that the Committee will confine its questioning to matters directly relevant to Andrew Gilligan's evidence. I understand that No.10 would be content with this approach.

Attached are drafts of the letters which the Defence Secretary proposes to send to Donald Anderson and Ann Taylor later today. I should be grateful for any comments that you may have by no later than 1430 today.

I am copying this letter to Jonathan Powell and Alastair Campbell (No.10) and to Sir David Omand and John Scarlett (Cabinet Office).

On 11 July Mr Hoon wrote to Mr Donald Anderson, the Chairman of the FAC, as follows:

Thank you for your letter of 10 July about Dr David Kelly.

I understand that Dr Kelly met Mr Gilligan on 22 May at about 1700 at the Charing Cross Hotel.

You also ask that Dr Kelly appears before the FAC on Tuesday 15 July at 1500. As you know, the Government has already suggested that the Intelligence and Security Committee (ISC) might wish to interview Dr Kelly as part of their continuing inquiry. (A copy of the MOD's press statement of 8 July is attached for convenience.) The Chairman of the ISC has now asked that Dr Kelly appears before them, also on next Tuesday, at 1230 for about 45 minutes. I am writing to Ann Taylor today agreeing to this request.

Although the FAC has now completed its own inquiry, I can understand why you also wish to see Dr Kelly. I am prepared to agree to this on the clear understanding that Dr Kelly will be questioned only on those matters which are directly relevant to the evidence that you were given by Andrew Gilligan, and not on the wider issue of Iraqi WMD and the preparation of the Dossier. Dr Kelly was not involved in the process of drawing up the intelligence parts of the Dossier.

As I noted above, Dr Kelly will have appeared earlier the same day before the ISC. I hope that you will bear this in mind and not detain him for longer than about the same period of time indicated by the ISC. As he is not used to this degree of public exposure, Dr Kelly has asked if he could be accompanied by a colleague. MOD officials will discuss this further with the Clerk.

I should be grateful if you could confirm that you are content to proceed on this basis.

On 11 July Mr Hoon wrote to Mrs Ann Taylor, the Chairman of the ISC as follows:

I understand that the Clerk has asked whether I would be content for Dr David Kelly to appear before the ISC on Tuesday 15 July at 1230 for about 45 minutes to give evidence about his meeting with Andrew Gilligan on 22 May. As the Ministry of Defence indicated in the statement it issued on Tuesday 8 July, there are no objections to Dr Kelly appearing.

I should point out that it is unusual for an MOD official of Dr Kelly's grade to appear as principal witness before the ISC. Given the exceptional circumstances, I am content for Dr Kelly to appear but I would not regard this as setting a precedent. I presume that Dr Kelly will be questioned only on those matters which are directly relevant to the claims made by Andrew Gilligan, and not on the wider issue of Iraqi WMD and the preparation of the Dossier on which you have already arranged to take evidence from a range of more senior and qualified witnesses. Dr Kelly was not involved in the process of drawing up the intelligence parts of the Dossier.

Dr and Mrs Kelly spent the 11 and 12 July at the house of friends in Cornwall.

On 11 July Dr Wells and Dr Kelly had a telephone conversation in which Dr Wells told Dr Kelly of the request that he should appear before the FAC and the ISC and Dr Kelly stated that he would be prepared to appear before both Committees although he expressed concern about the publicity which would arise from appearing before the FAC. He also requested that he should be accompanied by a colleague who should give him guidance on procedures, should that be required.

On 14 July Dr Kelly travelled to London where he met Dr Wells in the MoD. Dr Wells told Dr Kelly that the MoD would arrange hotel accommodation for him in London that night so that he would not have to travel up the next day from Oxfordshire to give evidence before the two Committees but Dr Kelly said that he would prefer to stay with his daughter in Oxford and would again travel up to London on the next morning. In the course of this discussion Dr Wells gave Dr Kelly a letter which Mr Hatfield had written to him dated 9 July stating that he had breached departmental guidelines on contacts with journalists, but that formal disciplinary proceedings would not be initiated. Mr Hatfield had given this letter to Dr Wells for him to give to Dr Kelly. The letter was in the following terms:

DISCUSSIONS WITH THE MEDIA

1. I interviewed you with your line manager, Dr Bryan Wells on Friday

4 July, about your letter to him of 30 June in which you described your contacts with the media in general and Andrew Gilligan in particular. I explained that your letter had serious implications since, on the basis of your own account, you appeared to have broken departmental regulations in having unauthorised and unreported conversations with journalists. Your conversation with Andrew Gilligan also appeared to be relevant to the controversy surrounding allegations made by Gilligan about the Government's September 2002 dossier WMD. This letter is not concerned with those wider aspects, although we discussed them during the latter part of the interview on 4 July and at a subsequent meeting on 7 July.

2. During our interview you clarified and expanded on what you had said in your letter of 30 June and I asked you a number of follow-up questions. At the end, I concluded that you had indeed breached departmental instructions on numerous occasions by having conversations with journalists which had been neither authorised by nor reported to the MOD press office. I accepted your assurance that in general these were essentially background, technical briefings and that on many – but not all – occasions you had consulted the FCO press office informally. In the case of Gilligan, you had had two arranged meetings (in February and May 2003) subsequent to your initial contact in the margins of an IISS seminar last September. You had not sought permission or advice prior to either of these meetings and, until your letter of 30 June, had not thought to report them subsequently.

3. As I made clear, these are serious breaches of standard departmental procedure and you were unable to give me any satisfactory explanation for your behaviour. Your contact with Gilligan was particularly ill-judged. Your discussion with him in May has also had awkward consequences for both yourself and the department which could easily have been avoided. I accept your assurance that these consequences were unforeseen and unintended and, in particular, that as you state in your letter you did not make any allegations or accusations about the prepa-

ration of the September 2002 dossier. I also concluded on the basis of your account that you had not divulged any classified or otherwise privileged information. On this basis, I have concluded that although your behaviour fell well short of the standard that I would expect from a civil servant of your standing and experience, it would not be appropriate to initiate formal disciplinary proceedings. You should, however, understand that any further breach of departmental guidelines in dealing with the media would almost certainly result in disciplinary action, with potentially serious consequences.

4. You should be absolutely clear that while you are working in the MOD you are required to seek explicit authority from your line manager and the MOD press office before agreeing to talk to journalists, even if there may be occasions when there may be advantage, additionally, in consulting the FCO. I would also urge you to be very cautious in any comments you might make at or in the margins of public seminars and the like. There is always the dangers (sic) that such remarks may be taken out of context.

5. I should also remind you that the possibility of disciplinary action could be reopened if any facts were to come to light which appeared to call into question the account and assurances that you gave to me.

6. I am sending a copy of this letter to Dr Wells as your line manager and a copy to Richard Scott at Dstl which will be placed on your personal file.

This letter in its unopened envelope was found in Dr Kelly's study in his home in Oxfordshire after his death. The police examined the letter and found none of Dr Kelly's fingerprints on the letter. Therefore it appears that Dr Kelly had not opened the envelope and had not read the letter.

After his discussion with Dr Wells, Dr Kelly attended a meeting with Mr Martin Howard, Dr Wells and Ms Heather Smith, a personnel officer in the MoD, to discuss his appearance before the FAC and the ISC. Dr Wells made a typewritten record of the meeting on 22 July which was as follows:

Present
Mr Martin Howard, DCDI
Dr David Kelly
Dr Bryan Wells, DCPAC
Ms Heather Smith, DGCP CHRO Cond/AD

1. Howard started the meeting by saying that he wanted to ensure that Kelly understood the procedures that the FAC and ISC were likely to following during their evidence sessions, and that he was comfortable with what was required of him. There was no question of the MOD seeking to impose Departmental lines: Kelly was free to tell his own story. Howard outlined the different bases on which the FAC and ISC were constituted, and their current interests in the Government's policy towards Iraq and WMD.

2. Howard then outlined the areas that the two Committees might be free to question Kelly. These were:
(a) his role in Government, and relationship with the media;
(b) his role in drawing up the Government's September 2002 Dossier;
(c) his meeting with Gilligan: what transpired, and why he subsequently decided to inform his line management;
(d) (for the ISC) his access to intelligence in general;
(e) (for the ISC) his access to intelligence on the '45 minute claim'.

Howard emphasised that the Committee's questioning in these areas would be eliciting essentially factual answers, and Kelly should feel free to give his own story. Kelly confirmed that he was happy about this.

3. Howard then outlined other areas where the Committees might probe, which were at the margins of what the Defence Secretary had defined when agreeing that the Committees could interview Kelly, but which were nevertheless hard to refuse. These areas were:

(a) what Kelly thought of Government Policy on Iraq. Kelly said that his was a matter for Ministers;

(b) whether Kelly thought he was Gilligan's source. Kelly asked if he could say 'I don't believe I am'; Howard replied that Kelly was free to decide how to answer this to his own conscience: the Department was not telling him what to say;

(c) what disciplinary action was being taken against Kelly. Kelly said that this was a matter for MOD.

4. Kelly asked what he might say about the issue of Uranium imports from Niger. Howard noted that Kelly had already said that in his meeting with Gilligan he had confined himself to repeating the IAEA observations on the matter. Kelly should feel free to repeat the same line if that was his position.

5. Howard asked Kelly about his contacts with Susan Watts; Kelly said that they had not spoken about the September Iraq Dossier.

6. Wells asked Kelly how he wanted to take forward his wish to be accompanied by a colleague to the FAC. Kelly replied that, on the basis of this present meeting, he did not feel the need to have a colleague alongside him. He was aware that Wells would be accompanying him to the evidence sessions.

7. At the end of the meeting, Kelly said that he would welcome the chance to see Howard later in the week or early the following, to discuss Howard's recent visit to Iraq. He (Kelly) was looking forward to returning to theatre (sic). Howard said he would be pleased to see Kelly, to discuss Iraq and for a general discussion after the evidence sessions. Kelly concluded by saying that he appreciated Howard's giving up so much time to discuss his appearances before the Committees.

Dr Wells' typewritten record made on 22 July was based on a handwritten note which he had made at the meeting on 14 July and his handwritten note contained the words 'tricky areas' which were not included in the typewritten record. A handwritten note made at the meeting by Dr Kelly also contained the words 'tricky areas' as did a handwritten note made at the meeting by Ms Heather Smith. It appears that the 'tricky areas' were the three areas set out in paragraph 3 of Dr Wells' typewritten record.

On the afternoon of 14 July Mr Gilligan sent an e-mail to Mr Greg Simpson, an official of the Liberal Democratic Party, in relation to Dr Kelly's appearance before the FAC on the next day and later in the afternoon Mr Simpson sent on that e-mail to Mr David Chidgey MP, a member of that party and a member of the FAC. The e-mail was in the following terms:

> We have been doing some research on David Kelly. Aside from the red herring of a source-hunt, he is an extremely interesting witness in his own right – probably, if he answers fully, the best you'll have had.
>
> He is described in one of the standard reference works (Tom Mangold and Jeff Goldberg, Plague Wars) as 'the senior adviser on biological warfare to the MoD ... the West's leading biological warfare inspector' with 'world-recognised expertise in every aspect of biological warfare [whose] knowledge cannot be overtrumped.
>
> As has been reported, he was the chief field inspector of UNSCOM, the predecessor to UNMOVIC. He led the first and last BW inspections in Iraq carried out by UNSCOM.
>
> He was one of three officials who accompanied Jack Straw when Straw gave evidence to the FAC about Iraq's WMD programmes on September 25 2002, one day after publication of the Blair dossier. He said hardly anything, however; Straw did all the talking.
>
> We believe he is currently the chief British inspector on the Iraq Survey Group (the No.2 Brit in the Group under Brigadier John Deverell, the British contingent commander.)
>
> Questions for Kelly
> What is the current state of the Iraq Survey Group's knowledge about Iraq's BW programme? Have you found anything? Did you believe in September 2002 that Iraq was an immediate danger? Was everyone

happy about the inclusion of the 45 minute point in the dossier in the light of what's been discovered since? Did you know the 45-minute point was single-source? Were there any arguments between the intelligence services and No 10 over the dossier?

Above all, he should be asked to say what kind of a threat Iraq was in September 2002 in his opinion. If he is able to answer frankly it should be devastating. Obviously he works for the Government and who pays the piper calls the tune. But if you could put some of these quotes (particularly the Watts) to him I think it would have some impact.

He is on record as saying that Iraq was NOT the greatest WMD threat. Leakage from the Russian programmes, he believed, was a greater threat.

For instance, CBC (Canadian TV), 23 October 2002: 'Leakage from Russia is the greatest threat, because Russia had a dedicated programme and a great understanding of how you use smallpox as a volatile weapon.'

On 18 Oct 2001, at the height of the US anthrax scare, Kelly told The Independent that if suspicion fell on any country as the source of the US anthrax 'the obvious one is Russia, it's a league ahead of Iraq.' He also said that Iraq had 'too much at stake' to take part in any action against the West.

He also told my colleague Susan Watts, science editor of Newsnight (who described him as ' a senior official intimately involved with the process of pulling together the dossier'):

'In the run–up to the dossier, the Government was obsessed with finding intelligence to justify an immediate Iraqi threat. While we were agreed on the potential Iraq threat in the future, there was less agreement about the threat the Iraqis posed at that moment.

That was the real concern – not so much what they had now, but what they would have in the future. But that unfortunately was not expressed strongly in the dossier, because that takes the case away for war to a certain extent ....

[The 45 minutes point] was a statement that was made and it got out of all proportion. They were desperate for information. They were pushing hard for information that could be released. That was one that popped up and it was seized on, and it's unfortunate that it was. That is why there is the argument between the intelligence services and No 10, because they picked up on it and once they'd picked up on it you can't pull it back from them ...So many people were saying 'well, we're not sure about that' ... because the word-smithing is actually quite important.'

Does he still agree with this?

Is Kelly our source? We are not ruling anyone in or out as the source. I had many conversations with people inside and outside the intelligence community about the issue of Iraqi WMD and the dossier. We suspect the MoD of playing games to try to eliminate names.

However: if, as the MoD has said, Kelly's involvement in the dossier was only tangential, he cannot be our source. Two of my source's claims which have proved to be true – that the 45-minute point derived from a single informant, and that it came in late – have been shown to be true. Such facts could only have been known to someone closely involved in compiling the dossier until a late stage.

It is clear that Mr Chidgey made use of the quotation of what Dr Kelly said to Ms Susan Watts set out in the e-mail when he questioned Dr Kelly the next day when he appeared before the FAC.

After breakfast Dr Kelly travelled up to London from Oxford and met Dr Wells in the MoD in the mid morning. It had been arranged that Dr Kelly would give evidence before the ISC in the Cabinet Office in Whitehall at noon on Tuesday 15 July and would give evidence before the FAC at 2.30pm on that afternoon. In the course of the morning the clerk to the ISC informed Mr Hoon's office that Dr Kelly's appearance before that Committee had to be postponed to the next day, but there was a misunderstanding about which hearing by a Committee had been postponed and Dr Kelly, accompanied by Dr Wells and Wing Commander John Clark, who was a friend and colleague of Dr Kelly in the MoD, went to the Cabinet Office and then returned to the

MoD on learning of the misunderstanding. In the afternoon Dr Kelly, accompanied by Dr Wells, Wing Commander Clark and Mrs Wilson, the chief press officer of the MoD went to the House of Commons and Dr Kelly gave evidence to the FAC.

The 15 July was an extremely hot day in London, a bomb scare in Whitehall prevented Dr Kelly being driven to the House of Commons in a government car as had been arranged, and he had to walk there in a rush. In his appearance before the FAC Dr Kelly gave the following evidence:

Q15 Mr Hamilton: May I ask which drafts of the final September dossier did you see and were drafts sent back to you at every stage for your comment?

Dr Kelly: No, I was not involved in that process at all.

Q16 Mr Hamilton: So you made your contribution and that went into it subsequently?

Dr Kelly: Yes. My contribution was not to the intelligence dimension.

Q17 Mr Hamilton: Can I ask what meetings you attended at which the dossier was discussed?

Dr Kelly: I attended no meetings at all at which the dossier was discussed.

Q18 Mr Hamilton: So you were asked to prepare a section?

Dr Kelly: I was.

Q19 Mr Hamilton: You prepared that section, you had access to the relevant intelligence material and that was submitted to the person compiling the dossier?

Dr Kelly: The component that I wrote did not require intelligence information, let us get that straight. It was not the intelligence component of the dossier, it was the history of the inspections, the concealment and deception by Iraq, which is not intelligence information.

Q20 Mr Olner: Dr Kelly, could you speak up, please. The problem is these microphones do not amplify the noise.

Dr Kelly: I apologise. I have a soft voice, I know.

Q21 Chairman: One final question under this heading. Presumably you did discuss this with other colleagues who were involved themselves in the preparation of the dossier, so you knew what was going on?

Dr Kelly: I was familiar with some of it. Actually I was either on leave or working abroad in the August and earlier September of that time frame. That component, no, I really was not involved.

Q22 Mr Chidgey: I just want to move on to the section of our inquiry dealing with contacts with Andrew Gilligan and journalists, but before we talk about Andrew Gilligan can I just confirm that you have also met Susan Watts?

Dr Kelly: I have met her on one occasion.

Q23 Mr Chidgey: Thank you. I would just like to read out to you a statement in the notes that were made: 'In the run-up to the dossier the Government was obsessed with finding intelligence to justify an immediate Iraqi threat. While we were agreed on the potential Iraqi threat in the future there was less agreement about the threat the Iraqis posed at the moment. That was the real concern, not so much what they had now but what they would have in the future, but that unfortunately was not expressed strongly in the dossier because that takes the case away for war to a certain extent'. Finally, 'The 45 minutes was a statement that was made and it got out of all proportion. They were desperate for information. They were pushing hard for information that could be released. That was one that popped up and it was seized on and it is unfortunate that it was. That is why there is an argument between the intelligence services and Number 10, because they had picked up on it and once they had picked up on it you cannot pull back from it, so many people will say 'Well, we are not sure about that' because the word smithing is actually quite important.' I understand from Miss Watts that is the record of a meeting that you had with her. Do you still agree with those comments?

Dr Kelly: First of all, I do not recognise those comments, I have to say. The meeting I had with her was on November 5 last year and I remember that precisely because I gave a presentation in the Foreign Office on Iraq's weapons of mass destruction. I cannot believe that on that occasion I made that statement.

Q24 Mr Chidgey: That is very helpful. Can I just be clear on this: I understand that these notes refer to meetings that took place shortly before the Newsnight broadcasts that would have been on 2 and 4 June.

Dr Kelly: I have only met Susan Watts on one occasion, which was not on a one-to-one basis, it was at the end of a public presentation.

Q43 Ms Stuart: I may not have heard something you said in response to Mr Chidgey's question. You did confirm that you had a meeting and talked with Susan Watts?

Dr Kelly: I have met with her personally once at the end of a seminar I provided in the Foreign Office on November 5.

Q44 Ms Stuart: You have neither met nor talked to her since?

Dr Kelly: I have spoken to her on the telephone but I have not met her face–to–face.

Q45 Ms Stuart: When have you talked to her on the telephone?

Dr Kelly: I would have spoken to her about four or five times.

Q46 Ms Stuart: During May at all?

Dr Kelly: During May? I cannot precisely remember. I was abroad for a fair part of the time in May, but it is possible, yes.

Q47 Ms Stuart: Have you had any conversations or meetings with Gavin Hewitt?

Dr Kelly: Not that I am aware of, no. I am pretty sure I have not.

...

Q56 Mr Olner: Really Mr Gilligan's story was basically about drafts of dossiers being changed, being 'sexed–up'. Did you infer to Mr Gilligan in any way, shape or form that he might have misrepresented what you said?

Dr Kelly: My conversation with him was primarily about Iraq, about his experiences in Iraq and the consequences of the war, which was the failure to use weapons of mass destruction during the war and the failure by May 22 to find such weapons. That was the primary conversation that I had with him.

Q57 Mr Olner: You certainly never mentioned the 'C' word that he went on to explain in his column?

Dr Kelly: The 'C' word?

Q58 Mr Olner: The Campbell word.

Dr Kelly: The Campbell word did come up, yes.

Q59 Mr Olner: From you? You suggested it?

Dr Kelly: No, it came up in the conversation. We had a conversation about Iraq, its weapons and the failure of them to be used.

Q60 Mr Olner: How did the word 'Campbell' come to be mixed up with all of that? What led you to say that?

Dr Kelly: I did not say that. What I had a conversation about was the probability of a requirement to use such weapons. The question was then asked why, if weapons could be deployed at 45 minutes notice, were they not used, and I offered my reasons why they may not have been used.

Q61 Chairman: Again, I am finding it very difficult to hear. The fans have been turned off, could you do your very best to raise your voice, please.

Dr Kelly: It came in in that sense and then the significance of it was discussed and then why it might have been in the dossier. That is how it came up.

Q62 Mr Pope: Mr Gilligan said in his article in the Mail on Sunday of 1 June 'I asked him', the source, 'how this transformation happened. The answer was a single word. 'Campbell'.' In your conversation with Mr Gilligan did you use the word 'Campbell' in that context?

Dr Kelly: I cannot recall using the name Campbell in that context, it does not sound like a thing that I would say.

Q63 Mr Pope: Do you believe that the document was transformed, the September dossier, by Alastair Campbell?

Dr Kelly: I do not believe that at all.

Q64 Mr Pope: When you met Mr Gilligan on 22 May he says in his article that he met a source in a central London hotel on that day. Did you meet him in a central London hotel?

Dr Kelly: I did.

Q65 Chairman: Which hotel was that?

Dr Kelly: The Charing Cross Hotel.

Q66 Mr Pope. Did you begin your conversation with Mr Gilligan by discussing the poor state of Britain's railways?

Dr Kelly: No.

Q67 Mr Pope: The reason I ask is because he said 'We started off by moaning about the railways' and what I am trying to get to the bottom of is whether or not you were the source, the main source, of Mr Gilligan or whether you were one of the other three minor sources which Mr Gilligan has told us he had. I am really trying to get to the bottom of that. Mr Gilligan will not answer this Committee's questions on those specific points. I just want to know, in your own opinion do you believe that you were the main source of Mr Gilligan's article on 1 June?

Dr Kelly: My belief is that I am not the main source.

Q68 Mr Pope: Do you know who the main source is?

Dr Kelly: No.

Andrew Mackinlay: Any idea?

Q69 Mr Pope: I want to be absolutely clear on this. You do not believe that you are the main source, that it is someone else?

Dr Kelly: From the conversation I had with him, I do not see how he could make the authoritative statement he was making from the comments that I made.

Q70 Mr Maples: Dr Kelly, just following on from what Mr Pope was saying. Mr Gilligan told us that he had four sources in this area and we are trying to find out whether you are the one or whether you are one of the other three.

Did you know about this 45 minute claim before the dossier was published?

Dr Kelly: No, it became apparent to me on publication.

Q71 Mr Maples: So you did not know about it before you, like all of us, read the dossier?

Dr Kelly: No. I might have appreciated it 48 hours beforehand but not before that.

Q72 Mr Maples: You would not have known about it significantly in advance. You were never part of any discussions about whether this should or should not be included in the dossier?

Dr Kelly: No.

...

Q101 Andrew Mackinlay: So you made no comments about the veracity of [the dossier] at all to Gilligan, you did not say it was exaggerated, embellished, probably over–egged?

Dr Kelly: No, I had no doubt that the veracity of it was absolute.

Q102 Chairman: Sorry, I had no doubts?

Dr Kelly: On the veracity of the document.

Q103 Andrew Mackinlay: Did you express any view about that document at all to him which you can share with this Committee?

Dr Kelly: We are talking of a conversation we had six weeks ago and for me it is very difficult to recall that, so I cannot recall the comments that I made. All I can say is that the general tenet of that document is one that I am sympathetic to. I had access to an immense amount of information accumulated from the UN that complements that dossier quite well, remarkably so, and although the final assessment made by the United Nations was status of verification documentation, not a threat assessment, the UN did not make a threat assessment, put the two together and they match pretty well.

Q104 Andrew Mackinlay: Okay. Dr Kelly, a few moments ago I asked you for the names of other journalists you have had contact with in the timescale we were talking about and you said you have not got access to your home. We are going to write formally to the MoD and by that time you will have done your homework and sent it to us in an envelope, but this afternoon can you tell me those journalists who you do recall having met in the timescale? What are their names?

Dr Kelly: Having met?

Q105 Andrew Mackinlay: Yes.

Dr Kelly: I have met very few journalists.

Q106 Andrew Mackinlay: I heard 'few', but who are the ones in your mind's eye at this moment? What are their names?

Dr Kelly: That will be provided to you by the Ministry of Defence.

Q107 Andrew Mackinlay: No, I am asking you now. This is the high court of Parliament and I want you to tell the Committee who you met.

Dr Kelly: On this occasion I think it is proper that the Ministry of Defence communicates that to you.

Chairman: But it is a proper question.

Andrew Mackinlay: You are under an obligation to reply.

Chairman: If you have met journalists there is nothing sinister in itself about meeting journalists, save in an unauthorised way.

Q108 Andrew Mackinlay: Who are they?

Dr Kelly: The only people that I can remember having spoken to in recent times about this particular issue – not about this particular issue – is Jane Corbin and Susan Watts.

Q116 Richard Ottaway: Dr Kelly, you confirmed in response to questions from Mr Pope that in your opinion you do not think that you were the central source of Mr Gilligan's report?

Dr Kelly: That is my belief.

Q117 Richard Ottaway: In Mr Gilligan's report there were two fundamental assertions which have subsequently been proved correct. One is that the 45 minute assertion was entered late into the September dossier and, secondly, that the 45 minute assertion came from a single, uncorroborated source. I think we can safely say from what you have been saying that you were unaware of either of those two things?

Dr Kelly: Correct.

Q118 Richard Ottaway: Given that Mr Gilligan's source of the story has proved to be correct, do you think it is fair to say that you could not have been the source? It is not jut a question of your opinion, but you could not have been the source.

Dr Kelly: It is very difficult for me to be that strong. I do realise that in the conversation that I had there was reinforcement of some of the ideas he has put forward.

Q119 Richard Ottaway: Given that there were two assertions which have been proved correct, which you did not know about, you clearly were not the source of those assertions.

Dr Kelly: Correct.

Q120 Richard Ottaway: So, therefore, you could not have been the central source?

Dr Kelly: Correct.

Q121 Richard Ottaway: When it was announced that the MoD put out a statement that you had been in contact with the press, in the penultimate paragraph the MoD says: 'We do not know whether this official is the single source quoted by Mr Gilligan'. Given what you have said today, why did you allow that statement to be made?

Dr Kelly: Can you repeat the statement, please?

Q122 Richard Ottaway: 'We do not know whether this official is the single source quoted by Mr Gilligan'.

Dr Kelly: Because I think that is the MoD's assessment.

Q123 Richard Ottaway: Did you know that they were going to say that?

Dr Kelly: I did.

Q124 Richard Ottaway: Did you tell them that it was an incorrect statement?

Dr Kelly: No. The whole reason why this has come up and the reason why I wrote to my line management was because I had a concern that because I had met with Andrew Gilligan in fact I may have contributed to that story. When I reflected on my interaction with him and realised the balance between the general conversation and the very specific aspect we are now discussing today, which was a very, very minor part of it, I did not see how on earth I could have been the primary source. I did not see how the authority would emanate from me.

Q125 Richard Ottaway: I share your analysis, I do not see how you could have been the primary source. Why did you not complain to the MoD that this was an inaccurate statement they were making?

Dr Kelly: Because, as I have just explained, I did realise that in fact I may have inadvertently, if you like, contributed to that.

Q126 Richard Ottaway: You reached the conclusion that you were not the source?

Dr Kelly: I do not believe I am the source.

Q127 Richard Ottaway: You have just concurred with me that you could not have been the source.

Dr Kelly: Following the logic I agree with that, yes.

Q128 Richard Ottaway: In that, the MoD says they do not know of the source and it was knowingly said by you.

Dr Kelly: That is the situation.

Q129 Richard Ottaway: Do you think possibly the MoD knowingly got it wrong?

Dr Kelly: No, I am saying that the MoD cannot make the categorical statement that you want it to make based on my information provided to them.

Q130 Richard Ottaway: I have to say that there seems to be an inconsistency between your two statements. Would you agree that there is an inconsistency between your belief that you were not the single source and the MoD's statement?

Dr Kelly: There is an element of inconsistency there, I have to agree with you.

Q131 Richard Ottaway: In response to my colleague, David Chidgey, he gave you a quote which appeared on Newsnight in a programme introduced by Susan Watts. You have confirmed that you have spoken to Susan Watts. Can I take you through the quote again that was read out. You said you did not recognise it. Could you just concentrate on it. It is talking about the 45 minute point. It said: 'The 45 minute point was a statement that was made and it got out of all proportion. They were desperate for information. They were pushing hard for information that could be released. That was the one that popped up and it was seized on and it is unfortunate that it was. That is why there is the argument between the intelligence services and Number 10, because they picked up on it and once they had picked up on it you cannot pull back from it, so many people will say 'Well, we are not sure about that' because the word smithing is actually quite important.' There are many people who think that you were the source of that quote. What is your reaction to that suggestion?

Dr Kelly: I find it very difficult. It does not sound like my expression of words. It does not sound like a quote from me.

Q132 Richard Ottaway: You deny that those are your words?

Dr Kelly: Yes.

...

Q155: Sir John Stanley: Who made the proposition to you, Dr Kelly, that you should be treated absolutely uniquely, in a way which I do not believe any civil servant has ever been treated before, in being made a public figure before being served up to the Intelligence and Security Committee?

Dr Kelly: I cannot answer that question. I do not know who made that decision. I think that is a question you have to ask the Ministry of Defence.

Q156 Sir John Stanley: So you did not make it yourself?

Dr Kelly: Certainly not.

Q157 Sir John Stanley: We have to assume therefore that your ministers then are responsible for treating you uniquely as a civil servant in highly publicising you before going to the Intelligence and Security Committee?

Dr Kelly: That is a conclusion you can draw.

Q158 Sir John Stanley: Why did you go along with it, Dr Kelly? You were being exploited, were you not?

Dr Kelly: I would not say I was being exploited.

Q159 Sir John Stanley: You had been before them to rubbish Mr Gilligan and his source, quite clearly?

Dr Kelly: I just found myself to be in this position out of my own honesty in acknowledging the fact that I had interacted with him. I felt obliged to make that statement once I realised that I may possibly be that source. Until then, I have to admit that I was out of the country for most of the time this debate was going on so I was not following the actual interactions that were going on. It was not until I was alerted to the transcript by a friend that I actually even considered that I might be the source.

Q160 Sir John Stanley: If I may say so, I think you have behaved in a very honourable and proper manner by going to your departmental line managers in the circumstances you describe. That does not get away from the key issue, which is why did you feel it was incumbent upon you to go along with the request that clearly had been made to you to be thrown to the wolves, not only to the media but, also, to this Committee?

Dr Kelly: I think that is a line of questioning you will have to ask the Ministry of Defence. I am sorry.

Sir John Stanley: I am grateful.

Q161 Chairman: Do you feel any concern at the way the Ministry of Defence responded after you volunteered your admission?

Dr Kelly: I accept what has happened.

Q162 Andrew Mackinlay: The feeling I have, and you might be able to help me with this, was that there was no serious attempt by the security or intelligence services or the Ministry of Defence Police to find out Gilligan's source. Did they come knocking at your door or that of your colleagues, to your knowledge at all, to discover that?

Dr Kelly: I have no knowledge of that whatsoever.

Q163 Andrew Mackinlay: Since you wrote to your superiors in the way you have done, have you met Geoff Hoon?

Dr Kelly: No.

Q164 Andrew Mackinlay: Any Ministers?

Dr Kelly: No.

Mr Pope: Any special advisers?

Q165 Andrew Mackinlay: Any special advisers?

Dr Kelly: No.

**Q166 Andrew Mackinlay:** Do you know of any other inquiries which have gone on in the department to seek the source – to clarify in addition to you or instead of you or apart from you?

None whatsoever?

**Dr Kelly:** No.

**Q167 Andrew Mackinlay:** I reckon you are chaff; you have been thrown up to divert our probing. Have you ever felt like a fall–guy? You have been set up, have you not?

**Dr Kelly:** That is not a question I can answer.

**Q168 Andrew Mackinlay:** But you feel that?

**Dr Kelly:** No, not at all. I accept the process that is going on.

**Q169 Chairman:** I am sorry. You accept...?

**Dr Kelly:** I accept the process that is happening.

**Q170 Mr Hamilton:** Dr Kelly, I am sorry to go back to something that I know you have already answered or partially answered, but I just want to clarify. My colleague, Mr Ottaway, did refer to this earlier. I just want to come back to this question of Alastair Campbell and Mr Gilligan. The MoD statement states that when Mr Gilligan asked about the role of Alastair Campbell with regard to the 45 minute issue 'he made no comment and explained that he was not involved in the process of drawing up the intelligence parts of the dossier' – that is you, of course. Just for the record, can you tell me absolutely whether you named or otherwise identified Alastair Campbell or did you say anything which Mr Gilligan might reasonably have interpreted as identifying Mr Alastair Campbell as wanting to change the dossier or 'sex it up' in any way or make undue reference to the 45 minute claim?

Dr Kelly: I cannot recall that. I find it very difficult to think back to a conversation I had six weeks ago. I cannot recall but that does not mean to say, of course, that such a statement was not made but I really cannot recall it. It does not sound like the sort of thing I would say.

...

Q172 Sir John Stanley: How do you explain the reasons for the delay between the letter you wrote on 30 June and the release of the Ministry of Defence statement throwing you to the wolves?

Dr Kelly: I cannot explain the bureaucracy that went on in between. I think it went through the line management system and went through remarkably quickly.

Q173 Sir John Stanley: Did you get any impression that the statement was delayed by the Ministry of Defence in order to ensure that it went out only after our report was published?

Dr Kelly: I cannot answer that question. I really do not know.

Q174 Mr Olner: You work for the MoD, Dr Kelly, but work obviously very closely with the intelligence and security services. Did you suggest to anyone at all that the intelligence and security services were unhappy about the September dossier?

Dr Kelly: Unhappy? I do not think they were unhappy. I think they had confidence in the information that was provided in that dossier.

Q175 Mr Olner: So there was no, if you like, feeling within the security services that this was a piece of work that had been 'sexed–up' and it was going to be rubbished at the end of the day?

Dr Kelly: I think there were people who worked extremely hard to achieve that document and the calibre of the document that was produced.

Q176 Mr Pope: When you met Mr Gilligan on 27 May did you feel at the time that you were doing anything untoward, that you were breaching the confidence that is expected of you within your job?

Dr Kelly: No. I think it has been agreed by the Ministry of Defence there was no security breach involved in the interactions I had.

Q177 Mr Pope: Do you think, in your experience, that there is a widespread culture in the MoD and, perhaps, in the intelligence and security services of people speaking in an unofficial capacity to journalists? Certainly the impression I got from Mr Gilligan was that that was a widespread culture that journalists would have a number of contacts in the MoD or in the security services. Is that your experience?

Dr Kelly: It is not my experience but I think you have to recognise that I have a strange background in the sense that I operated for ten years internationally interacting with international press and was well-known to the press and had quite a lot of contact. I think I am somewhat unusual in terms of the people who have an interest in that situation.

Q178 Mr Pope: Finally, were you aware of any widespread unease about the accuracy of the September dossier, at the time it was published, amongst people who were involved in providing information for it?

Dr Kelly: I do not believe there was any difficulty over the accuracy of that document.

In his evidence Wing Commander Clark was asked if Dr Kelly had said anything to him in the afternoon after he had given evidence to the FAC. Wing Commander Clark's evidence was:

Q. Did Dr Kelly comment on any of the questions that he had been asked?

A. Yes. He was totally thrown by the question or the quotation that was given to him from Susan Watts. He spoke about that when he came back to the office. He did say that threw him. He had not expected or anticipated that that would have come to the fore at that forum.

Q. When you say the question about Susan Watts, can you be a bit more precise about what that questions was?

A. I cannot remember exactly which member of the Committee, but a member of the Committee read out a very long quotation from Susan Watts – well, no, it was a quotation that had been reported on by Susan Watts which apparently David or Dr Kelly had said. Now, in response to that Dr Kelly said it was not his quote. That had come on quite early. That had really surprised him, that that quote had been tabled to him.

Q. So after the hearing he says to you: that really threw me?

A. Yes he did.

Q. Did he say why it really threw him?

A. No, I have no recollection of that.

On 15 July 2003, after the FAC had heard evidence from Dr Kelly, the Chairman of the Committee, Mr Donald Anderson, wrote to Mr Jack Straw and stated:

> As you know, the Committee heard oral evidence today from Dr David Kelly of the Ministry of Defence.
>
> The Committee deliberated after hearing Dr Kelly's evidence, and asked me to write to you, expressing their view that it seems most unlikely that Dr Kelly was Andrew Gilligan's prime source for his allegations about the September dossier on Iraq. Colleagues have also

asked me to pass on their view that Dr Kelly has been poorly treated by the Government since he wrote to his line manager, admitting that he had met Gilligan.

I am copying this letter to Geoff Hoon and to Bruce George.

This letter was released to the press.

In response to the letter from Mr Anderson the MoD issued the following statement on the evening of 15 July:

The Foreign Affairs Committee has said that it seems most unlikely that Dr David Kelly was Andrew Gilligan's 'prime' source for his allegations.

As was made clear in our statement of 8 July, the MoD does not know whether Dr Kelly is the 'single' source referred to by Andrew Gilligan before the FAC.

The FAC use the phrase 'prime' source. Does this mean that the FAC doubt Mr Gilligan's story? If Dr Kelly is not the source, why does the BBC not say so now? The BBC has the opportunity to clear up this issue. Their silence is suspicious. Their appeal to the principle of source protection is clearly bogus in this case, as Dr Kelly came forward voluntarily.

We also note the FAC's view that Dr Kelly has been 'poorly treated' by the Government. We do not accept this. Dr Kelly came forward voluntarily with information on a matter of public interest. He has been properly treated in accordance with Departmental procedures. He has expressed no complaint to us or the FAC, who took the initiative to call him as a witness.

On 16 July the Clerk of the FAC wrote to the Private Secretary to Mr Hoon:

At his appearance yesterday before the Foreign Affairs Committee, Dr David Kelly was asked to supply a list of journalists with whom he has had contact. He pointed out that he will be unable to answer this question immediately, because he does not at present have access to his personal diaries. The Committee accepted that its question should be pursued through MoD.

I would be grateful to receive the information for which the Committee has asked as soon as you are able to supply it, accepting that it may be necessary to consult the transcript in order to confirm exactly what was sought. I will try to ensure you receive a copy of the transcript as soon as possible after it has been received in this office, which I expect to be either later today or early tomorrow.

On the morning of Wednesday 16 July Dr Kelly travelled up to London from Oxford and gave evidence before the ISC and he was accompanied by Dr Wells and Wing Commander Clark.

In his appearance before the ISC Dr Kelly gave (inter alia) the following evidence:

MICHAEL MATES: If you have a long history of dealing with the press and are an officer of the Ministry of Defence and understand that you are experienced in doing this and doing it on a regular basis what is then the difference to person like you to having an authorised meeting with him and an unauthorised meeting, surely in the olden days you didn't get authority every time you spoke to a person of the press?

DR KELLY: Yes. The situation is that in the very early days I only spoke to the press, either when they approached me in the Middle East when I had, I just had to react to it there and then, or if I was either in the United Kingdom or the United States at the behest of the United Nations, the Ministry of Defence and the Foreign Office. As time went by, of course, you have follow-up questions, you'd have clarification, individual reporters, individual companies, media companies would have my contact details and of course I would be contacted directly, and I'd use my discretion as to whether I responded to that or responded to which ever Ministry or Agency demanded and essentially that's what I've done ever since, I have used my discretion. Now as the years have gone by, of course, I've got 'cold calls' sometimes I've been asked about things which I haven't been dealing with before and again I used my judgment.

MICHAEL MATES: But specifically it has been, has it got this wrong, the MoD said that your contact with Andrew Gilligan was 'unauthorised'.

DR KELLY: That's correct.

MICHAEL MATES: But then doesn't the MoD expect you to use your judgment about these things or is there an absolute prohibition?

DR KELLY: I think in practice there's an absolute prohibition, but I also believe that of course there is an element of reality in all of this, and although there's an absolute prohibition, technically, in terms of the guidance that is provided one.

MICHAEL MATES: And on the occasions when you have spoken to the press, and it has been known you've spoken to the press, because for whatever reason have you been reprimanded?

DR KELLY: This is the first time I've ever got into any trouble.

ANN TAYLOR: Is it that the first, because it was the first time you've done something that is so clearly unauthorised, or is it because it's the first time it's been a problem?

DR KELLY: I think it's the first time it's been a problem! ...

...

DR KELLY: I was aware of the general debate that was going on between those who were supporting the war and those who were against the war and the justification for war and I saw this as being part of that debate. The reference was to a senior intelligence officer who'd been involved, primarily in drafting the dossier, that didn't match me, I'm not an intelligence officer, I was not involved, I mean I was involved in aspects of drafting the dossier but in the non-intelligence dimension but I certainly wasn't responsible for the final content of that dossier, so the alarm bells didn't start ringing. A friend of mine at RUSI suggested, and I don't think she suggested because she identified me, but she said I should read that, and when I read it there was one phrase in there that I read as being a 'Kelly' statement, which was a statement about the probability that Iraq had, the probability was that Iraq had chemical weapons and that probability was about 30%. That is something that I say and so I then re-read it and thought 'well is this what I've been saying all the way through' and I think there is a blend of what I have said and what someone may have said.

MICHAEL MATES: You've said always that the probability is 30% that they had chemical weapons?

DR KELLY: The probability is 100% that they had a programme and I think it's about 30% that they have chemical weapons.

MICHAEL MATES: And you said that too, to Gilligan?

DR KELLY: I said that to many people.

...

MICHAEL MATES: And, just the last point, are you surprised at the public MoD reactions or was it that the statement made with your agreement?

DR KELLY: The official MoD press statement was made with my agreement, yes.

MICHAEL MATES: So you weren't surprised, okay.

ANN TAYLOR: Can I just ask before I move on to James, you mentioned the transcript of the FAC and you said that you weren't an intelligence officer and that whilst you were involved in drafting the dossier you weren't involved in the applying or editing or decisions on it, do you thinks that Andrew Gilligan regarded you as an intelligence officer and did you at any stage tell him that you'd been involved in the drafting or the writing about this document, or information for it?

DR KELLY: I've not acknowledged to anyone that I was involved in the drafting of the dossier, I meant, that essentially, my component which was the non-intelligence component which was done at the request of the Foreign Office so not even Brian Wells' predecessor as the Director of PAC was aware that I wrote that part …

…

JAMES ARBUTHNOT: May I ask, the allegation that Andrew Gilligan made that someone had said that the forty-five minutes, that the issue of forty-five minutes was over-hyped in the document. That's not something that you recognised as having come from you?

DR KELLY: No I think I may well have said that the forty–five minute mention was there for impact, yes, because it came out of a conversation, not about the dossier, but about Iraq, 'why weapons had not been used and why they had not been found subsequently' and then the question was 'well if you have something that is available in forty-five minutes surely it would have been used' and then, I can't identify such a system that you could use within forty-five minutes and then the question was 'why would it be included' and I can't give an answer as to why it would be included?

JAMES ARBUTHNOT: So if you might have said that it was there for impact, you can't be firmer than that as to whether you did or did not say that it was there for impact?

DR KELLY: No I'm pretty sure I said it was there for impact, I've acknowledged that.

MICHAEL MATES: As opposed to being factually correct?

DR KELLY: It depends on how you interpret what I've said. I have said that I don't, I can't identify a weapons system that could be used within forty-five minutes of deployment.

MICHAEL MATES: To Gilligan?

DR KELLY: Yes, I've said it to many people, but to Gilligan, yes.

JAMES ARBUTHNOT: So if that was a statement that was there for impact was it a statement that you think should not have been there?

DR KELLY: I think I'd like to quote Hans Blix who at the weekend said that he thought it was unwise to have it there, I think that's probably the correct statement to make. I can't, I really can't say that I thought it should not be there because I'm actually not aware of the intelligence behind it.

JAMES ARBUTHNOT: But you did feel that it unwise to it there?

DR KELLY: Now I do, yes. At the time, when it came out, I really didn't make a judgment on it, it was there, it was a statement, I was puzzled but it by I didn't make a judgment on it.

JAMES ARBUTHNOT: Did you think when you were speaking to Andrew Gilligan that you gave him the impression that you felt it was unwise for it to have been there?

DR KELLY: That's a possibility, I can't, really can't, because you are talking about a dynamic and I really can't recall … I have to admit it's a possibility, yes.

JAMES ARBUTHNOT: Did you or he mention Alastair Campbell in your discussions in May?

DR KELLY: Alastair Campbell came up – because the question was then 'well why was it there?' and he asked that question, now I was not involved in the process of assembling the dossier, my contribution to the dossier was in May/June of last year, after that I had no involvement in the compilation of the dossier, the drafting of it, the synthesis of it, so I was not in a position to comment on that.

JAMES ARBUTHNOT: So when he said 'why was it there?' what did you say, if you can remember?

DR KELLY: I can't recall accurately because, but, I mean essentially it would be words to the effect that I could not comment, I really cannot remember the exact phrase that I used because I was not in a position to comment.

JAMES ARBUTHNOT: Might it have been that you said, you said Alastair Campbell came up in the context of 'why was it there?'; How did Alastair Campbell come up in the context of that?

DR KELLY: I'm having great difficulty to clearly remember this, but my feeling is the question was asked by Gilligan.

JAMES ARBUTHNOT: What question?

DR KELLY: When you asked about 'why it was there' and then the successive question was about Campbell.

JAMES ARBUTHNOT: So might Andrew Gilligan have said, did Andrew Gilligan say 'why was it there?' and then did he say 'was it Campbell who put it in'.

DR KELLY: I mean that's the sequence that occurred, I mean the exact phrasing I regret I cannot remember, on this occasion this was not something of deep significance to me, you have to remember and so …

JAMES ARBUTHNOT: But if he had said 'was it Campbell who put it in' what do you think you would have said in reply?

DR KELLY: Well I would have no knowledge of that, I just did not have any knowledge about that, so I could not have responded positively or negatively for that matter.

GAVIN STRANG: Could I just ask you know, what is your view of that September dossier?

DR KELLY: My view of the dossier?

GAVIN STRANG: Yes, standing back a bit and giving a view based on your experience and knowledge of that subject.

DR KELLY: I think it is an accurate document, I think it is a fair reflection of the intelligence that was available and it's presented in a very sober and factual way. It's presented in a way that is not an intelligence document or a technical document, I think it is presented in a way that can be consumed by the public, it is well written.

GAVIN STRANG: And you think that precisely what's there will stand the test of time?

DR KELLY: Yes I think so and of course there are certain features that have been confirmed, the extended range missiles, UNMOVIC have found certain weapons albeit not many of them which were capable of dealing either chemical or biological materials so that, to a certain extent has been substantiated, but I'd have to admit that the substantiation is quite small at the moment.

ANN TAYLOR: Just as a follow–up to that, what level of understanding of the document did you think that Andrew Gilligan had when you were discussing these matters with him?

DR KELLY: We didn't really discuss the dossier, the conversation I had was about Iraq and many aspects of that, it came up in the context of weapons, whey they had not been used, why they'd not been found; and in the course of that discussion the question came up about why the forty–five minutes was there, when that came into the dossier, and for me, I mean it's very difficult now to know whether it was a fleeting moment, whether it was two minutes, three minutes, I really can't recall, it may be that he was focused on that issue, but I certainly wasn't I was more focused on acquiring information about Iraq immediately post–conflict which would be useful to my work in the future.

ALAN HOWARTH: You said to us that you thought that there was an absolute prohibition on a person in your position talking to the media, but you suggested that this more or less happens more as a notion than absolute prohibition. Were you in breach of normal practice in doing what you did?

DR KELLY: My understanding now is that I was in breach of normal practice.

ALAN HOWARTH: But you weren't aware at the time that you were in breach of normal practice?

DR KELLY: No, because essentially on this, I actually very rarely meet journalists although I do talk to them on the telephone and on this occasion, I must admit, I'd regarded it more as being more a private conversation than I had a briefing or in any way a disclosure at all.

ALAN HOWARTH: And you didn't report back to any colleagues on the fact of your conversation and what had been said.

DR KELLY: No.

ALAN HOWARTH: When you went to meet Andrew Gilligan, at the Charing Cross Hotel, did you enter the discussion with an agenda of your own, you've mentioned that you were anxious to learn what you could from him, but did you also go to meet him with a view to conveying any particular points to him.

DR KELLY: No, it was very much with the intention of being in receive mode

– to understand his experience he had in Iraq.

ALAN HOWARTH: So did you feel justified in talking to him as you did at the time?

DR KELLY: I felt comfortable, I'm not sure what you mean by justified.

ALAN HOWARTH: Do you still feel comfortable about the fact that you did so?

DR KELLY: Had this not all have arisen then yes I would have, because I actually did derive information from him, which was useful. I of course deeply regret it, with hindsight, but yes, if this had not arisen it would have been a useful meeting for me.

ALAN HOWARTH: And you regard him as a reliable witness, you've derived information from him, are you satisfied as to the quality, reliability of what you learned from him?

DR KELLY: I am, the information that I derived from him which I found interesting was that he was actually accessing individuals who had not surrendered and he visited them at their homes, he did not physically gain access to them, which was surprising to me, first of all, was that he knew where they were and apparently the Security Services didn't, whether they did or not, and were eavesdropping, I just don't know, and that those individuals were being protected by the regime, or the residue of the regime and so I found that quite fascinating as to why particular individuals would be protected in such a way.

ALAN HOWARTH: And do you know how to take good advantage of such contacts?

DR KELLY: I don't know is the answer to that. They are people that he had apparently had spoken to before the war.

JOYCE QUIN: Can I ask you how you respond to the letter that the Chairman of Foreign Affairs Committee has apparently written to the Foreign Secretary expressing the view that it seems most unlikely that you were Andrew Gilligan's prime source for his allegation about the September dossier on Iraq.

DR KELLY: Well that's what I believe myself, I mean I do not believe that I'm the prime source, regrettably I've discussed with him issues that are – now – controversial, but I did not do that, my instigation that I raised, it was not something that I felt particularly strongly about, and people who know me know that I feel quite strongly that Iraq had weapons programmes, that they had such weapons and my whole background working for both the Ministry of Defence and the United Nations really supports the position of the dossier, and one of the comments I made yesterday to the Foreign Affairs Committee was that in essence you take a report produced in 1999 by Richard Butler, which was a status of verification achieved by UNSCOM and put that alongside the dossier, they match quite well and the two together essentially comprise quite a reasonable definition of the problem, the threat presented by Iraq, and I also hasten to add that it was not of course the UN's job to do a threat assessment, it was very much a status of verification, but you can read that in another way, assess it as a threat.

JOYCE QUIN: When you volunteered the information to the MoD that you had met Andrew Gilligan did you at that time feel you might be the prime source, or again did you just come forward with that information because you felt it was better given that Andrew Gilligan's story was getting such prominence that you ought to make it clear that you had met him?

DR KELLY: I felt uncomfortable with the situation that I found myself in and so the only way of resolving that problem, because I thought, for three days before deciding to write, and my conscience dictated that I communicated what I had done in the best way that I could, and that's exactly what I did ...

...

ANN TAYLOR: Do you think that the dossier was a sound document?

DR KELLY: Yes ...

...

ALAN BEITH: In the course of the discussion it was assumed you would have people of your level of technical knowledge of these things, were you conscious that there were other people who shared your very, very specific reservations, that is for example that you couldn't conceive a weapon system which could have fitted this description or who voiced other reservations about either the dossiers or the general drift of government statements about Iraq?

DR KELLY: Three very different questions. My discussions are primarily technical, I think in terms of the latter part, no, I didn't discuss that with anyone, it wouldn't be my remit or interest to do so. In terms of the forty-five minutes, yes that was very seriously discussed, particularly with people in the United Nations, in UNMOVIC who were desperately trying to think about what system is it they should be looking for when they went back into Iraq, because it doesn't fit any of the known Iraqi systems, so yes, that was talked about and discussed very seriously.

ALAN BEITH: And with that kind of discussion very understandably, particularly UNMOVIC or ex-inspector colleagues, was that, did that in any way fit the description of 'turbulence in the system' which for example Pauline Neville-Jones used although she was presumably talking primarily about intelligence work, that is, which I interpret to be a lot of people having a lot of discussions are saying 'oh, we've got serious doubts about this or that'.

DR KELLY: I wouldn't describe it as 'turbulence in the system' when the people that I talked to when one was seriously trying to think about what it can refer to, and of course it stimulated talk about the systems that we know about as well, it was a serious discussion, I wouldn't describe it as 'turbulence', it's the sort of vigour of discussion you'd have as a consequence of a statement that's not well understood.

ALAN BEITH: Seen as an 'unconcluded' discussion.

DR KELLY: So far, yes ...

...

KEVIN BARRON: ...Did Gilligan have a pencil and paper with him, when you were chatting?

DR KELLY: He had a notebook with him, yes ...

...

JOYCE QUIN: And in the transcript of Gilligan's – in the final segment he said the words of his source were that it was transformed in a week before it was published to make it 'sexier', that didn't come from you then?

DR KELLY: The word 'transformed' is not something that would have occurred to me in terms of the document, first of all I had not seen the earlier drafts of it, so I wouldn't know whether it had been transformed or not, the document itself is a very sober, well written, there is no emotive language in it, it's factual, I don't see it as being 'transformed'.

MICHAEL MATES: But you wouldn't describe it as 'sexy'?

DR KELLY: I think the 'forty-five minutes' for impact is the only, that's the only bit that that would be the case.

JAMES ARBUTHNOT: But 'sexier' is that a word you would use?

DR KELLY: It is a word I would use, I use it on occasions.

JAMES ARBUTHNOT: Is it a word you did use?

DR KELLY: I cannot recall on that occasion.

JAMES ARBUTHNOT: But you might have done?

DR KELLY: It's possible, yes ...

...

ANN TAYLOR: Can I ask, at the beginning you mentioned that you do see certain intelligence reports but you haven't been very specific about that, can you give us some idea of what you see by way of JIC papers, what you see from DIS, you mentioned that you did see some intelligence reporting could you give us a fuller picture please, of what they might be?

DR KELLY: Certainly. I see all the *intelligence* reporting concerned with both Iraq and ***, with regard to chemical and biological weapons, that arrives in the Proliferation and Arms Control Secretariat and I have full access to that. Within the Defence Intelligence Services I liaise with the Rockingham cell which used to service UNMOVIC and UNSCOM and now will service the Iraq Survey Group and I don't go through all the information that they have but, almost on a weekly basis I'll sit down with the principal officer there and he will alert me to anything that he thinks is of relevance to my work. I also liaise with SIS, they call me in if they want to discuss any raw intelligence with me in if they want any assistance in interpreting intelligence. I see them every two months or so.

Prior to Dr Kelly's appearance before the FAC on 15 July Mr Andrew Mackinlay MP, a member of that Committee, had tabled two Parliamentary Questions for answer by the Secretary of State for Defence.

The first Parliamentary Question was:

To ask the Secretary of State for Defence, when over the past two years

Mr David Kelly has met Andrew Gilligan of the BBC.

The second Parliamentary Question was:

> To ask the Secretary of State for Defence, which journalists Mr David
> Kelly has met over the past two years; other than Andrew Gilligan of
> the BBC, (a) for what purpose each meeting was held, (b) when each
> meeting took place.

Dr Kelly was aware of these Parliamentary Questions before he went back to
Oxford from London on the afternoon of 16 July and it had been arranged that
on the next day, working from home, Dr Kelly would send the necessary
details to the MoD before 10am on 17 July to enable answers to be prepared to
those Questions. On Thursday 17 July at 9.22am Dr Kelly sent the following e-
mail to Wing Commander Clark and Dr Wells:

> John and Bryan,
>
> I have compiled the information as best I can. The list of journalists is
> the most difficult because some may date before 2002 and some may
> have nothing to do with Iraq whatsoever! Attached is the information
> in Word.
>
> Regards,

Attached to this e-mail was the following information:

> IISS meeting was 12 to 14th September 2002
> I have records of meeting:
> Nick Rufford (*Sunday Times*) 14th March 2002 (discussing Al–Manal)
> Alex Nicholl (*Financial Times*) 15th May 2002 (Iraqi WMD in general)
> Phillip Sen (*The Engineer*) 3rd October 2002 (Inspection technology)
> (Other than Andrew Gilligan I know that I have met Jane Corbin and
> Tom Mangold in the past year but have not recorded those meetings in

my diary.)

Letter to Peter Watkins

I have contact with the following journalists:

Tamar Weinstein, CBC Radio Canada

Anna Maria Tremonti, CBC Radio Canada

Bernard Edinger, Reuters

Andrew Veitch, ITN

Mark Worthington, TBS News

Tetsuya Chikushi News, 23 TBS News

Koichiro Yoneda, TBS News

Paul Lashmar, *The Independent*

Susan Lambert, Australian Broadcasting Corporation

Jeremy Webb, *New Scientist*

James Bone, The *Times*

Marilyn Chase, *Wall Street Journal*

Jeff Goldberg, Freelance journalist

Tom Mangold, BBC Panorama

Judith Miller, *New York Times*

Calum Lynch, *Washington Post*

Nick Rufford, *Sunday Times*

Helen Vyner, Simon Prentice Associates

Susan Wells, BBC[1]

Carolyn Hawley, BBC

Lynsey Hilsum, Channel Four News

Jane Corbin, BBC

Stephen Endelberg, *New York Times*

Sean O'Neill, *Daily Telegraph*

(note this is essentially a list of those journalists that I have business cards for or have recorded in my electronic contacts list, some may date from earlier than 2002; I will have had contact with others but I have no record).

On the morning of Thursday 17 July about 8.30am Dr Wells' office received four Parliamentary Questions tabled by Mr Bernard Jenkin MP.

The first Parliamentary Question was:

> To ask the Secretary of State for Defence, whether his Department has complied with Dr David Kelly's terms and conditions of employment in handling the matter of his discussions with Andrew Gilligan.

The second Parliamentary Question was:

> To ask the Secretary of State for Defence, on how many occasions Dr David Kelly spoke to BBC radio 4 defence correspondent Andrew Gilligan; and whether his line managers were aware of this.

The third Parliamentary Question was:

> To ask the Secretary of State for Defence, what (a) civil service and (b) MoD rules and regulations may have been infringed by Dr David Kelly in talking to BBC radio 4 defence correspondent Andrew Gilligan.

The fourth Parliamentary Question was:

> To ask the Secretary of State for Defence, what disciplinary measures his Department will take against Dr David Kelly.

At 9.28am on 17 July Mr James Harrison, Dr Wells' deputy, sent these four Parliamentary Questions to Dr Kelly attached to an e-mail which stated:

> David
>
> more PQs! But plenty of time for reply. I expect that Bryan will deal tomorrow.
>
> James

After receipt of Dr Kelly's e-mail sent at 9.22am, Wing Commander Clark helped to draft replies to the two Parliamentary Questions tabled by Mr Andrew Mackinlay and to the letter dated 15 July from the Clerk of the FAC requesting details of Dr Kelly's contacts with journalists. These replies were seen by the Parliamentary Under-Secretary's office which contacted Wing Commander Clark and suggested (inter alia) that as Ms Susan Watts had been referred to in the hearing when Dr Kelly appeared before the FAC, her name should be taken out of the general list of journalists to whom Dr Kelly had spoken and put into the paragraph which referred to the specific contacts that Dr Kelly had had with journalists. Accordingly Wing Commander Clark prepared a draft reply to the letter from the Clerk of the FAC dated 16 July which referred to a meeting with Ms Susan Watts on 5 November 2002.

Wing Commander Clark was asked what conversations he had had with Dr Kelly in the course of 17 July:

Q. Can you recall what conversations you had with Dr Kelly in the course of the 17th July apart from specifically on the e-mails?

A. Yes. We had a number of calls. The first one was obviously about 10 o'clock in the morning to say the information required is on the Internet machine. The reason he would make that call is the Internet machine is a stand alone machine in an office some 30 yards from where I work, so you had to know it was on there to go and find it.

We also had a general discussion of developments, how he was feeling. He was feeling still tired but in good spirits.

Q. Did you discuss going back to Iraq at all?

A. Yes, it was something we discussed regularly because Dr Kelly was very keen to get back to Iraq to support the ISG and on that morning, because we thought that really we were clearing the workload associated with PQs and with the Select Committees, we looked at a reasonable date for him going back. Having discussed it with Dr Wells, we came up with the date of the 25th which basically gave him just slightly over a week to get his personal effects sorted out and then he would fly out. So that – I spoke to him on the Thursday and it was going to be a week the following Friday that he would fly out.

Q. Did you book a flight for him?

A. Yes, I did. Having agreed that then he was booked on a flight.

LORD HUTTON: So that was a definite plan, Wing Commander, was it, that he would go out on the 25th?

A. It was my Lord.

LORD HUTTON: He knew that?

A. Provided basically we would seek authority from the Deputy Chief of Defence Intelligence that he was happy we had received it, it was a definite plan. He had agreed that Dr Kelly himself could easily make that date.

During the course of 17 July Wing Commander Clark was also contacted by the Private Secretary to Mr Hoon who referred to an article written by Mr Nick Rufford in the Sunday Times on 13 July referring to Dr Kelly. Dr Kelly had made no reference to that meeting with Mr Rufford in the details he had given of meetings with journalists and Wing Commander Clark was asked to check with Dr Kelly if that meeting had taken place and, if it had, to include it in the reply. Wing Commander Clark telephoned Dr Kelly to speak to him on this point about 3.20pm. His evidence was:

Q. At what time did you attempt to ring Dr Kelly?

A. It was – I have since been told by the police – I thought it was close to 3 o'clock but it was about 3.20, and I was told by his wife who answered the telephone that Dr Kelly had gone for a walk at 3 o'clock.

Q. Can you recall what the last telephone conversation you actually had with Dr Kelly was before that attempt to get hold of him?

A. Yes, I had a call with him which was just before 3 o'clock. Again I thought it was earlier but we have been able to track that down from investigating my log of e–mails and the telephone log that the police were able to provide. So about 6 or 7 minutes before 3 o'clock was the last conversation. That was the one where we discussed Susan Watts and the business cards.

Q. When you say Susan Watts, i.e. appearing in the body of the text?

A. Absolutely right. So that had been agreed.

On the morning of 17 July at 11.18am Dr Kelly sent a number of e-mails to friends and colleagues who had sent him, by e-mail, messages of support. To Ron Manley:

> Ron

> Many thanks for your thoughts. It has been difficult. Hopefully it will all blow over by the end of the week and I can travel to Baghdad and get on with the real work.

> Best wishes

> David.

> To Geeta Kingdon:

> Geeta,

> Many thanks for your thoughts and prayers. It has been a remarkably tough time. Should all blow over by early next week then I will travel

to Baghdad a week Friday.

I have had to keep a low profile which meant leaving home for a week!
Back now.

With best wishes and thanks for your support.

David

# Chapter 5

*On the morning of 18th July the body of Dr Kelly was found by a footpath near to his home.*

On Sunday 20 July the BBC issued the following statement:

> The BBC deeply regrets the death of Dr David Kelly. We had the greatest respect for his achievements in Iraq and elsewhere over many years and wish once again to express our condolences to his family.
>
> There has been much speculation about whether Dr Kelly was the source for the Today programme report by Andrew Gilligan on May 29th. Having now informed Dr Kelly's family, we can confirm that Dr Kelly was the principal source for both Andrew Gilligan's report and for Susan Watts reports on Newsnight on June 2nd and 4th.
>
> The BBC believes we accurately interpreted and reported the factual information obtained by us during interviews with Dr Kelly.
>
> Over the past few weeks we have been at pains to protect Dr Kelly being identified as the source of these reports. We clearly owed him a duty of confidentiality. Following his death, we now believe, in order to end the continuing speculation, it is important to release this information as swiftly as possible. We did not release it until this morning at the request of Dr Kelly's family.
>
> The BBC will fully co-operate with the Government's inquiry. We will make a full and frank submission to Lord Hutton and will provide full details of all the contacts between Dr Kelly and the two BBC journalists including contemporaneous notes and other materials made by both journalists, independently.
>
> We continue to believe we were right to place Dr Kelly's views in

the public domain. However, the BBC is profoundly sorry that his involvement as our source has ended so tragically

# Chapter 6

The Issues

In my opinion my terms of reference require me to consider a number of issues which arise from the evidence which I have summarised in the preceding paragraphs of this report. They are issues which counsel addressed in their examination and cross-examination of witnesses and in their statements at the conclusion of the evidence. The issues may be grouped under five main headings:

I Issues relating to the preparation of the dossier of 24 September 2002.

II Issues relating to Dr Kelly's meeting with Mr Gilligan in the Charing Cross Hotel on 22 May 2003.

III Issues relating to the BBC arising from Mr Gilligan's broadcasts on the BBC Today programme on 29 May 2003.

IV Issues relating to the decisions and actions taken by the Government after Dr Kelly informed his line manager in the MoD that he had spoken to Mr Gilligan on the 22 May 2003.

V Issues relating to the factors which may have led Dr Kelly to take his own life.

I am satisfied that Dr Kelly took his own life and that the principal cause of death was bleeding from incised wounds to his left wrist which Dr Kelly had inflicted on himself with the knife found beside his body. It is probable that the ingestion of an excess amount of Coproxamol tablets coupled with apparently clinically silent coronary artery disease would have played a part in bringing about death more certainly and more rapidly than it would have otherwise been the case. I am further satisfied that no other person was involved in the death of Dr Kelly and that Dr Kelly was not suffering from any significant mental illness at the time he took his own life.


Summary of conclusions on the issues relating to the preparation of the dossier of 24 September 2002

The conclusions which I have come to on these issues are the following:

The dossier was prepared and drafted by a small team of the assessment staff of the JIC. Mr Scarlett, the Chairman of the JIC, had the overall responsibility for the drafting of the dossier. The dossier, which included the 45 minutes claim, was issued by the Government on 24 September 2002 with the full approval of the JIC.

The 45 minutes claim was based on a report which was received by the SIS from a source which that Service regarded as reliable. Therefore, whether or not at some time in the future the report on which the 45 minutes claim was based is shown to be unreliable, the allegation reported by Mr Gilligan on 29 May 2003 that the Government probably knew that the 45 minutes claim was wrong before the Government decided to put it in the dossier was an allegation which was unfounded.

The allegation was also unfounded that the reason why the 45 minutes claim was not in the original draft of the dossier was because it only came from one source and the intelligence agencies did not really believe it was necessarily true. The reason why the 45 minutes claim did not appear in draft assessments or draft dossiers until 5 September 2002 was because the intelligence report on which it was based was not received by the SIS until 29 August 2002 and the JIC assessment staff did not have time to insert it in a draft until the draft of the assessment of 5 September 2002.

The true position in relation to the attitude of 'the Intelligence Services' to the 45 minutes claim being inserted in the dossier was that the concerns expressed by Dr Jones were considered by higher echelons in the Intelligence Services and were not acted upon, and the JIC, the most senior body in the Intelligence

Services charged with the assessment of intelligence, approved the wording in the dossier. Moreover, the nuclear, chemical and biological weapons section of the Defence Intelligence Staff, headed by Dr Brian Jones, did not argue that the intelligence relating to the 45 minutes claim should not have been included in the dossier but they did suggest that the wording in which the claim was stated in the dossier was too strong and that instead of the dossier stating 'we judge' that 'Iraq has:- military plans for the use of chemical and biological weapons, including against its own Shia population. Some of these weapons are deployable within 45 minutes of an order to use them', the wording should state 'intelligence suggests'.

Mr Campbell made it clear to Mr Scarlett on behalf of the Prime Minister that 10 Downing Street wanted the dossier to be worded to make as strong a case as possible in relation to the threat posed by Saddam Hussein's WMD, and 10 Downing Street made written suggestions to Mr Scarlett as to changes in the wording of the draft dossier which would strengthen it. But Mr Campbell recognised, and told Mr Scarlett that 10 Downing Street recognised, that nothing should be stated in the dossier with which the intelligence community were not entirely happy.

Mr Scarlett accepted some of the drafting suggestions made to him by 10 Downing Street but he only accepted those suggestions which were consistent with the intelligence known to the JIC and he rejected those suggestions which were not consistent with such intelligence and the dossier issued by the Government was approved by the JIC.

As the dossier was one to be presented to, and read by, Parliament and the public, and was not an intelligence assessment to be considered only by the Government, I do not consider that it was improper for Mr Scarlett and the JIC to take into account suggestions as to drafting made by 10 Downing Street and to adopt those suggestions if they were consistent with the intelligence available to the JIC. However I consider that the possibility cannot be completely ruled out that the desire of the Prime Minister to have a dossier which, whilst consistent with the available intelligence, was as strong as possible in relation to the threat posed by Saddam Hussein's WMD, may have subconsciously influenced Mr Scarlett and the other members of the JIC to make the wording of the dossier somewhat stronger than it would have been if it had been contained in a normal JIC assessment. Although this possibility cannot be completely ruled out, I am satisfied that Mr Scarlett, the other members of the JIC, and the members of the assessment staff engaged in the drafting of the dossier were concerned to ensure that the contents of the dossier were consistent with the intelligence available to the JIC.

The term 'sexed-up' is a slang expression, the meaning of which lacks clarity in the context of the discussion of the dossier. It is capable of two different meanings. It could mean that the dossier was embellished with items of intelligence known or believed to be false or unreliable to make the case against Saddam Hussein stronger, or it could mean that whilst the intelligence contained in the dossier was believed to be reliable, the dossier was drafted in such a way as to make the case against Saddam Hussein as strong as the intelligence contained in it permitted. If the term is used in this latter sense, then because of the drafting suggestions made by 10 Downing Street for the purpose of making a strong case against Saddam Hussein, it could be said that the Government 'sexed-up' the dossier. However in the context of the broadcasts in which the 'sexing-up' allegation was reported and having regard to the other allegations reported in those broadcasts I consider that the allegation was unfounded as it would have been understood by those who heard the broadcasts to mean that the dossier had been embellished with intelligence known or believed to be false or unreliable, which was not the case.

Issues relating to Dr Kelly's meeting with Mr Gilligan in the Charing Cross Hotel on 22 May 2003

These issues are the following:

What did Dr Kelly say to Mr Gilligan in the course of the meeting?
At the time of his meeting with Mr Gilligan and discussing the dossier with him was Dr Kelly having a meeting which was unauthorised and in breach

of the Civil Service rules of procedure which applied to him?

At the time of the meeting or subsequently to it did Dr Kelly realise that the meeting was unauthorised and in breach of the Civil Service rules of procedure which applied to him?

Summary of conclusions on the issues relating to Dr Kelly's meeting with Mr Gilligan in the Charing Cross Hotel on 22 May 2003

The conclusions which I have come to on these issues are the following:

In the light of the uncertainties arising from Mr Gilligan's evidence and the existence of two versions of his notes made on his personal organiser of his discussion with Dr Kelly on 22 May it is not possible to reach a definite conclusion as to what Dr Kelly said to Mr Gilligan. It may be that Dr Kelly said to Mr Gilligan that Mr Campbell was responsible for transforming the dossier, and it may be that when Mr Gilligan suggested to Dr Kelly that the dossier was transformed to make it 'sexier', Dr Kelly agreed with this suggestion. However I am satisfied that Dr Kelly did not say to Mr Gilligan that the Government probably knew or suspected that the 45 minutes claim was wrong before that claim was inserted in the dossier. I am further satisfied that Dr Kelly did not say to Mr Gilligan that the reason why the 45 minutes claim was not included in the original draft of the dossier was because it only came from one source and the intelligence agencies did not really believe it was necessarily true. In the course of his evidence which I have set out, Mr Gilligan accepted that he had made errors in his broadcasts in the Today programme on 29 May 2003. The reality was that the 45 minutes claim was based on an intelligence report which the Secret Intelligence Service believed to be reliable and the 45 minutes claim was inserted in the dossier with the approval of the Joint Intelligence Committee, the most senior body in the United Kingdom responsible for the assessment of intelligence. In addition the reason why the 45 minutes claim was not inserted in the first draft of the dossier was because the intelligence on which it was based was not received by the SIS in London until 29 August 2002. Therefore the allegations reported by Mr Gilligan that the Government probably knew that the 45 minutes claim was wrong or questionable and that it was not inserted in the first draft of the dossier because it only came from one source and the intelligence agencies did not really believe it was necessarily true, were unfounded.

Dr Kelly's meeting with Mr Gilligan was unauthorised and in meeting Mr Gilligan and discussing intelligence matters with him, Dr Kelly was acting in breach of the Civil Service code of procedure which applied to him.

It may be that when he met Mr Gilligan, Dr Kelly said more to him than he had intended to say and that at the time of the meeting he did not realise the gravity of the situation which he was helping to create by discussing intelligence matters with Mr Gilligan. But whatever Dr Kelly thought at the time of his meeting with Mr Gilligan, it is clear that after Mr Gilligan's broadcasts on 29 May Dr Kelly must have come to realise the gravity of the situation for which he was partly responsible by commenting on intelligence matters to him and he accepted that the meeting was unauthorised, as he acknowledged in a telephone conversation with his friend and colleague Ms Olivia Bosch after his meeting with Mr Gilligan.

Issues relating to the BBC arising from Mr Gilligan's broadcasts on the BBC Today programme on 29 May 2003
    These issues are the following:

(1) Was there a failure by the BBC to exercise proper editorial control over Mr Gilligan's broadcasts on the Today programme on 29 May?
(2) Was the BBC management at fault in failing to investigate properly and adequately the Government's complaints that the report was false that the Government probably knew that the 45 minutes claim was wrong even before it decided to put it in the dossier?
(3) Was there a failure by BBC management to inform the Governors of the BBC of the extent of editorial concerns about Mr Gilligan's broadcasts in relation to the 45 minutes claim?

(4) Whilst the Governors were under a duty to protect the independence of the BBC from Government interference, were the Governors at fault in failing to investigate properly and adequately the Government's complaints about the report on the Today programme in relation to the 45 minutes claim, and were the Governors too ready to accept the opinion of BBC management that the broadcasts were proper ones for the Today programme to make.

Consideration of the issues relating to the BBC

Having considered the evidence given by the witnesses from the BBC (leaving aside the evidence given by Mr Gilligan) I consider that the BBC was at fault in a number of respects as follows:

(1) I have already stated that the BBC failed to ensure proper editorial control over Mr Gilligan's broadcasts on 29 May and, in particular, over his first broadcast at 6.07am.

(2) I consider that the BBC management was at fault in failing to investigate properly and adequately the Government's complaints that the report was false that the Government probably knew that the 45 minutes claim was wrong even before it decided to put it in the dossier, in the following reports. The BBC management failed, before Mr Sambrook wrote his letter of 27 June to Mr Campbell, to make an examination of Mr Gilligan's notes on his personal organiser of his meeting with Dr Kelly to see if they supported the allegations which he had reported in his broadcast at 6.07am. When the BBC management did look at Mr Gilligan's notes after 27 June it failed to appreciate that the notes did not fully support the most serious of the allegations reported in the 6.07am broadcast, and it therefore failed to draw the attention of the Governors to the lack of support in the notes for the most serious of the allegations. A factor which contributed to these failures was the failure of the BBC management to appreciate the gravity of the allegations reported in Mr

Gilligan's broadcast at 6.07am and I consider that the allegations made against the Government in the broadcast at 6.07am were so grave and gave rise to such a serious public controversy that it was unreasonable for the BBC management to expect the Government to pursue its complaint about them through the usual channels of the BBC Programme Complaints Unit or the Broadcasting Standards Commission, procedures which could take weeks or, perhaps, months before a conclusion was arrived at. These failures are shown in the evidence of Mr Dyke, Mr Sambrook and Mr Davies.

Mr Dyke said:
[15 September, page 148, line 22]

A. On 25th and 26th June I was chairing a BBC – we have twice a year a BBC Executive Committee conference, this was in Surrey – when the news came through of a pretty ferocious attack which Alastair Campbell had launched not just against the particular report broadcast by Andrew Gilligan, but on the BBC's journalistic integrity and in particular on our coverage of the war.

Q. Your coverage of the?

A. Of the war, sorry.

Q. And what was your reaction to that?

A. Well, I discussed it with Richard Sambrook who was also at the conference. He had been invited by that time to appear on the Today Programme the following day to answer Mr Campbell's allegations and we both agreed that he should leave the conference and go. I mean, an attack of this sort of scale from the Government's Director of Strategy and Communications was pretty near unprecedented, I would have thought.

LORD HUTTON: Had you, by this stage, read the details of Mr Gilligan's broadcast report on 29th May, Mr Dyke?

A. (Pause). I do not remember.

LORD HUTTON: Yes.

A. I think probably not.

LORD HUTTON: Yes.

A. Probably not.

LORD HUTTON: You see, I have read already part of the report which said that actually the Government probably knew that the 45 minutes figure was wrong even before it decided to put it in. Would you regard that as a very grave charge indeed against the Government?

A. Well, of course it – it was a charge being made not by the BBC but by a source to the BBC; but at that stage I would not have read that. I would have received Stephen Whittle's account of our process. The process was going pretty well. I would have talked about this with Richard Sambrook. By this time remember the story had died away. This had not been brought on to our radar screen over the previous 10 days at all, 14 days.

LORD HUTTON: Whether the charge was made by the BBC or by a source which the BBC was reporting, would you regard it as a very serious allegation?

A. Oh, it is pretty serious charge. But there is a distinction between a charge made by the BBC and a charge made by a source to the BBC.

LORD HUTTON: Yes.

A. They are very – a very different – they carry a different degree of gravity.

...

[15 September, page 157, line 2]

Q ... When you were helping draft [Mr Sambrook's letter of 27 June in reply to Mr Campbell's letter of 26 June], did you, at that stage, listen to a tape of the broadcast on 29th May?

A. (Pause). I think we read the transcript.

Q. You read the transcript. I think we have that at BBC/1/5 onwards. What was your reaction, if we look at BBC/1/4, to the opening of the piece which Mr Gilligan has told us was unscripted and had followed a more neutral introduction by the news reader?

A. Well, I think we – during that day we had all the transcripts of not just the early piece, but we had all the different pieces that were run throughout the morning; and I read through them. What I did was to largely get involved in the writing of the first half of the reply.

Q. Right. But having read, for example, this bit at BBC/1/4 where it was said 'the Government probably knew that the 45 minute figure was wrong', I can take you to other bits later on.

A. Sure. I cannot say that particular piece jumped out at me. I mean, clearly we knew there were fairly serious allegations, the point has been made, but I do not think that piece particularly jumped out.'

Mr Dyke, referring to the drafting of Mr Sambrook's reply to Mr Campbell dated 27 June, said:

[15 September, page 161, line 6]

Q. Did you ask or were you shown, at this stage, Mr Gilligan's notes of his meeting?

A. No.

Q. Were they available to the meeting that was drafting this reply?

A. No. Mr Gilligan was there, but – he was in the part of the meeting in the other part of the office, he was not at the meeting where I was. But we assumed that these replies were accurate.

LORD HUTTON: Why did you assume they were accurate, Mr Dyke? I mean very strong protests were being made by the Government on this particular point and the Chairman of the Joint Intelligence Committee had said that the report was wrong. Now, why did you not consider the accuracy of it?

A. Because we were reporting a source. I mean, there is a real distinction, and it has been, I think, muddled in a lot of the reporting, including I would say some of our own reporting of this issue.

MR DINGEMANS: Will you explain the distinction?

A. The distinction was whether this was the BBC saying this or whether this was the BBC reporting the source. We were reporting a source. There are questions that have to be asked when you are doing that, but that work had been done and the view was that this was a credible source to report.

Mr Sambrook said:

[17 September, page 110, line 17]

Q. Can I, please, just move on to some matters involving you rather more closely? The reply to Mr Campbell's substantially long letter of complaint of 26th June was, in part, drafted by you?

A. It was, yes.

Q. Do you accept that there were some errors in that letter [of 27 June] as to what Dr Kelly had in fact said to Mr Gilligan?

A. Yes, I do.

Q. Had you looked at Mr Gilligan's notes at the time that you drafted that reply?

A. No, I had not, no.

Q. Do you accept, with hindsight, that you should have done?

A. Yes, I think if I had been able to go through Andrew Gilligan's notes in some detail and gone through them with him in some detail, we might have got to a point where we realised these were not comments that were directly attributable to Dr Kelly; and clearly I regret that.

Q. Was Mr Gilligan involved in the drafting process of that letter?

A. Yes, he was.

Q. I do not think we need turn the passages up, but did Mr Gilligan consent to the letter going out in the form that it did?

A. Yes he did. Indeed, part of the reason why Mr Gilligan spent most of that day in our offices, as the letter was being drafted, was that he could be consulted on matters such as that.

...

[17 September, page 122, line 3]

Q. Would you agree that the more serious the allegation, the greater the care which you would expect the BBC to take to ensure that it can be properly supported?

A. Yes.

Q. These were exceptionally serious allegations, were they not?

A. Well, I think one thing I should make clear is that I do not think the programme or indeed the BBC, in those early weeks, ever took the wording of the 6.07 broadcast or that phrase within the 6.07 broadcast to be the definitive version of the allegations that we were making. I think our view was the definitive version was the scripted version, in the news bulletins at 6 o'clock, 7 o'clock and 8 o'clock and at 7.32. The live two-ways at 6 o'clock are deemed by the programme, although it is certainly true the audience does not necessarily perceive them this way, as a sort of preview for the major reports that are coming up during that day's programme. So I think the mindset on the programme, and I think this continued for some time afterwards, was that the definition of this item, in the BBC's view, were the scripted versions of it and the 6.07 was something that had strayed from what we believed to be the core allegations we were making or that our source was making.

Q. Leaving aside the mindset of the programme, you very fairly accept the audience would not necessarily have perceived it the same way?

A. Indeed.

Q. In practice it is the most dramatic and gravest allegation which will attract the most attention rather than the allegation which is scripted?

A. Depending on how often it is repeated and how many people hear it, yes.

Q. Yes. But if you make a sufficiently dramatic allegation, other media will catch on to it, will they not?

A. They may do, yes.

Q. They are professional followers of each other's copy, are they not?

A. They are.

Q. Now, you have already I think agreed in your earlier evidence, and indeed I think it is implicit in the evidence you have given today, that the 6.07 allegation that the Government probably knew that the 45 minutes point was wrong before putting it into the dossier was, in fact, going to strike people as an exceptionally grave allegation. I think you have accepted that?

A. It clearly had that effect.

Q. Yes. It was an attack, was it not, on its face, on the integrity of those who had been involved at the highest levels in the production of the dossier?

A. In the way it was phrased, it clearly would have had that effect. It is a different question about intent.

Q. Yes, I understand that. Even in the 7.32 broadcast, the allegation was, was it not, that the Government had put the 45 minute point into the dossier against the advice of the Intelligence Services, who had told them that they regarded it as questionable?

A. Words to that effect, yes.

...

[17 September, page 160, line 8]

Q. Mr Dyke has given evidence and you I think have associated yourself this afternoon with that evidence, to virtually quote him, I think, that he wished that he had paused in late June and ordered a full investigation of the whole issue.

A. Yes.

Q. That is one of the points that Mr Dyke made which you associate yourself with?

A. I certainly think we should have paused and considered at greater length the charges that were being levelled against us. Whether that amounts to a full investigation of the whole issue, I am not sure. But I certainly think the letter of the 27th was written under considerable pressure, particularly the deadline imposed on us by Mr Campbell, and if we had not been under that pressure to respond then the errors in that letter of the 27th might not have been made.

Q. There was not in fact a careful examination of all the allegations that had been made, how far they could be supported by Mr Gilligan's notes and what conclusions should be drawn from that before the Governors' meeting, was there?

A. There was an investigation and examination. What we did not do was go through the personal organiser notes in point by point detail with Andrew. If we had done that, I think it might have pointed up the two errors that we made in that letter. But we certainly went through every point that Mr Campbell raised in his letter. We discussed them in some detail, both with Andrew Gilligan and with Kevin Marsh, and we just discussed them between ourselves as a senior editorial team before coming out with that letter. I would not want anybody to think that the letter was written purely in haste. We spent as much time as we had over it and we went into considerable detail on all the points that Mr Campbell made.

Q. The truth is that the investigation that had been carried out by the time the Governors met on 6th July was no fuller than the investigation that had been made before you wrote that letter, except in this respect: that you had, by now, looked at both versions of Mr Gilligan's notes?

A. We had seen Mr Gilligan's notes, that is true. We had also, by that time, identified many similarities in Ms Watts' reports as well with the reports Andrew Gilligan had made, which had taken us some time to get to because I was abroad when her broadcasts originally went out. I think that also lent some support to the broad thrust of the allegations that Mr Gilligan's source was making.

Q. In the press release following the meeting of the Governors, it was said that the BBC had never attacked the good faith of the Prime Minister.

A. That is also what I said in my Today interview on the 26th.

Q. Did anyone draw the Governors' intention to what Mr Gilligan had in fact said at 6.07?

A. No, it was not at the forefront of our minds. Indeed, it was not at the forefront of our minds in drafting the response of the 27th because it was raised there by Mr Campbell for the first time, as the third of those 12 questions, and indeed in the previous three letters from the Government the wording of the 6.07 broadcast had never been referred to you (sic) and their complaints were much more about whether we had abided by the producer guidelines, the strength given to denials and a number of other issues, such as the description of the JIC. They had never drawn the precise language of the 6.07 as being the core of their complaint. Indeed, even when we got the letter of the 26th where it was raised for the first time in that list of questions, I took the core of their complaint to be that John Humphreys paragraph on the front page.

Q. So nobody said, as I understand your evidence, to the Governors at that meeting: there is a problem about the 6.07 broadcast, which was unscripted, and where Mr Gilligan appears to have gone further than he should have done?

A. No, because at that time the Government's complaint was all-encompassing. They were not saying: we have a problem, we have a complaint about the 6.07 broadcast. They said: we have a complaint about the entirety of these allegations. I think Mr Campbell's letter to the Director General on the 26th said 'the story is 100 per cent wrong'. This was an all or nothing complaint, not a complaint about a phrase in one version of 19 broadcasts.

Q. It was a number of complaints, one of which related specifically to the 6.07 broadcast.

A. I accept that the wording of the 6.07 was raised for the first time in the letter of the 26th, yes.

Q. In fact you had at 6.07, whether you intended to or not, attacked the good faith of the Government, had you not?

A. On reflection I can see that. At the time, I do not think that was sufficiently recognised, no.

Q. Did anyone point out to the Governors that the dossier had said that it reflected the views of the JIC and Mr Gilligan had broadcast, at 7.32, an allegation that the Government had actually inserted things contrary to intelligence advice? Was that point made to the Governors?

A. No. As I have explained to you before, we saw the core allegations that were being made about the scripted items rather than 6.07, and again, even in that allegation we did not accept that the reservations of the Intelligence Services necessarily referred to the heads of those services or the JIC; and I believe we always thought of it in terms of people lower down the chain who had been involved in the assessment and production of the dossier, who were concerned, and at some level unspecified in the BBC's broadcast, that stuff had been included against their advice.

LORD HUTTON: May I just ask you on that point, Mr Sambrook, if we look at BBC/1/4, which is the first page of the transcript, if we can scroll down that, please. Yes, just there. You see the paragraph there beginning: 'Well, erm, our source says that the dossier, as it was finally published, made the Intelligence Services unhappy ...' Then if we go over to the next page which is the com-

mencement of the broadcast at 7.32, about halfway down that passage: ' ...
Andrew Gilligan has found evidence that the Government's dossier on Iraq
that was produced last September was cobbled together at the last minute with
some unconfirmed material that had not been approved by the Security Services.' Now, there is a reference to the Intelligence Services being unhappy and
then there is a reference to 'had not been approved by the Security Services'.

A. Hmm.

LORD HUTTON: I think later there is a reference at 006 to Mr Gilligan, where
he said 'most people in intelligence were not happy'; but if one looks at the first
two references, that gives the picture, does it not, that it was the entirety of the
Intelligence Services, or would it not apply certainly to the heads of the Intelligence Services?

A. I accept that reading can be taken from it.

LORD HUTTON: You say 'can be taken from it'. Is that not the only reading
if you just look at those passages? Once they were heard by someone listening
to the broadcast: 'the Intelligence Services'.

A. I think all I can say, my Lord, is that in the programme's mind, and indeed
in ours for some time, that was not what we believed to be the allegation that
had been made.

LORD HUTTON: Is the important thing not what the listeners take it to
mean?

A. I agree with that, yes.

LORD HUTTON: Yes.

MR SUMPTION: You have accepted that there was no basis in Mr Gilligan's
notes for the assertion that that point had been made to him by Dr Kelly, the

conscious misfeasance point.

A. It was not in his notes, yes.

Q. Was that point made to the Governors?

A. Yes, I said to the Governors that his notes were not verbatim, were not – not every that he had broadcast was contained in his notes but that Mr Gilligan asserted that what was not there was a proper reflection of his conversation with Dr Kelly. The one point the Governors challenged me on was whether the name 'Campbell' was represented in the notes and I told them that it was, next to a phrase about transformation of the dossier. And that was really the only point that they wanted to have more clarification about the notes on.

Q. You see, Mr Sambrook, when you wrote the 27th June letter you had not seen Mr Gilligan's notes; and when you subsequently saw them you realised that there might be a problem about the unequivocal way in which you had answered Mr Campbell's question whether the BBC stood by the 6.07 allegation.

A. When I saw his notes I had the conversation with Andrew about those elements of his broadcast which were not captured in his notes and he continued to assert that his conversation with Dr Kelly backed up those comments, and I took him at face value.

Q. So he continued to tell you that that was what Dr Kelly had actually told him?

A. He continued to say it was a proper – he did not say it was a direct quote at that point but he did say it continued to be a proper reflection and interpretation of what Dr Kelly had told him, which is what I think I said in my evidence on the 13th.

Mr Davies said:

[24 September, page 29, line 9]

Q. Well, were you aware, at the time of the meeting, that Mr Sambrook had not examined Mr Gilligan's notes at the time of writing his letter on 27th June?

A. I was aware of that. I also knew he had written the letter in the presence of Mr Gilligan for a large part of his writing.

Q. Were you aware he had examined them since writing that letter?

A. I was aware he had examined them before the Governor's meeting.

Q. Were you aware the notes did not support the most serious of the allegations, namely Mr Gilligan's source had accused the Government of putting material into the dossier knowing it was probably wrong?

A. None of the Governors were aware that the notes did not substantiate that, and nor did, I think – was Mr Sambrook aware of that. He had looked at the notes and he had not, I think, picked up – I believe he said this to the Inquiry – that parts of the 6.07 broadcast were not repeated in the notes formally. However, he had asked the journalist, Mr Gilligan, whether or not he fully stood by the reports and the answer was, 'Yes, both factually and in terms of interpretation', and that is what he told us.

Q. So Mr Sambrook had looked at the notes but had not picked up the fact that the most serious of the allegations was not reflected in the note; that is your evidence, as I understand it, indeed it is Mr Sambrook's.

A. I think it was not repeated verbatim in the notes. I think Mr Sambrook had not noted that it was not repeated verbatim in the notes. I believe Mr Sambrook told the Inquiry that.

Q. The notes were not, of course, put before the Governors even in redacted form, were they?

A. No, they were not.

(3) The e-mail sent by Mr Kevin Marsh to Mr Stephen Mitchell on 27 June 2003 set out in paragraph 284 was critical of Mr Gilligan's method of reporting and was clearly relevant to the complaints which the Government was making about his broadcast on 29 May. Yet it appears that this e-mail of 27 June 2003 was never brought to the attention of Mr Sambrook or to the attention of the Governors. In his evidence Mr Dyke said:

[15 September, page 169, line 17]

Q. We have also seen an e-mail at BBC/5/118, in which comments were made about Mr Gilligan's reporting.

A. Yes.

Q. Did you see this e-mail?

A. No, I did not know of the existence of this e-mail until the day the Inquiry started. I should explain, I was away – I took a truncated holiday and therefore I came back and that was the first I knew of this e-mail.

LORD HUTTON: Do you think you should have been made aware of it before the Governors' meeting?

A. I do not think – my understanding, but you must confirm it with him, is that Richard Sambrook had not seen this e-mail before the Governors' meeting.

LORD HUTTON: Do you think he should have seen it?

A. There are a million e-mails a day inside the BBC. Unless somebody had referred it to him, he would not have seen it. But I certainly had not seen it; and I did not see it until the Inquiry started.

LORD HUTTON: But it is very critical of the broadcast about which the Government was making very serious complaints and about which there was a very serious controversy.

A. Sorry, can I just ... (Pause). It says this – yes, it makes – it expresses certain concerns: 'This story was a good piece of investigative journalism marred by flawed reporting.'

LORD HUTTON: 'Our biggest millstone has ...'

A. Yes, on reading this I could not say I was not concerned.

LORD HUTTON: If I could ask you again Mr Dyke: do you not think that somebody in the BBC chain of management should have brought this to the attention of Mr Sambrook and/or yourself before the Governors' meeting?

A. They would not have brought it to my attention.

LORD HUTTON: Very well, that -

A. This is further down the chain, quite a long way down the chain.

LORD HUTTON: Yes.

A. But, well – whether they should have done, they did not.

In his evidence Mr Sambrook said:

[17 September, page 132, line 6]

Q. We have certain observations from Mr Marsh himself which are included in an e-mail on 27th June which you will find at BBC/5/118. When did you first see this e-mail?

A. When it was disclosed for the Inquiry.

Q. I see. Now, as I understand it, partly from documents and partly from Mr Dyke's evidence, Stephen Mitchell is somebody who, from time to time, looks into matters which one might loosely call regulatory for the senior executives; is that wrong?

A. No, Stephen Mitchell is the head of Radio News who reports to me. It is Stephen Whittle who is the controller of editorial policy.

Q. You are right to correct me on that. If we could look at what Mr Marsh says: 'Some thoughts – clearly I have to talk to Andrew Gilligan early next week. I hope that by then my worst fears – based on what I'm hearing from the spooks this afternoon – aren't realised. Assuming not, the guts of what I would say are: 'This story was a good piece of investigative journalism, marred by flawed reporting – our biggest millstone has been his loose use of language and lack of judgment in some of his phraseology. 'It was marred also …' that is a point about the *Mail on Sunday* and the *Spectator*. 'That is in many ways a result of the loose and in some ways distant relationship he's been allowed to have with Today.' Have you discussed with Mr Marsh his views as reflected in this document?

A. I had discussed, before this document, in broad terms his views of Andrew Gilligan as a reporter and indeed with Stephen Mitchell as well, yes.

Q. Can you tell us why it is, what is the loose language which Mr Marsh is drawing attention to as possibly fulfilling his worst fears?

A. I am not sure that the loose language is related to the worst fears. I think that is a separate point.

Q. Leaving the fears, let us concentrate on the loose language.

A. As I said, this was not flagged up to me at the time. I only knew about it after it was disclosed to this Inquiry. My understanding of what Kevin was talking about is we should have had a consistent phrase for capturing the allegations that Dr Kelly was making, both for presenters and for reporters and within the report scripts, and it would have been a lot better if we had been entirely consistent on that.

Q. You had not seen this document, as I understand your evidence, by the time you briefed the Governors' meeting on 6th July?

A. That is correct.

Q. Do you think you should have done?

A. I think if Kevin Marsh or Stephen Mitchell had had real concerns about the nature of the reporting or indeed about the nature of the way we were dealing with the Government's complaint, I would have expected them to bring those to my attention. I am not clear that this e-mail necessarily represents serious concerns.

LORD HUTTON: You think it does not represent serious concerns?

A. My personal view about it is that it is much more saying – it is entitled 'from here'; my personal view about it is that it is an e-mail from a programme editor to his line manager saying that in future we would be better to have a more disciplined use in terms of scripting materials and not doing live two-ways and so on; and it is an attempt to look forward at how things should be managed in the future. Again, this was not flagged up to me at the time. All I can say is that, I mean, I know both Kevin Marsh and Stephen Mitchell extremely well and I believe if they had serious concerns about the quality of the journalism or indeed our response to the Government, they would have raised it directly with me and they did not.

MR SUMPTION: Is it not a source of concern if grave allegations are made against public figures on the basis of loose use of language and lack of judgment in the phraseology? Is that not a source of concern?

A. If that is their view then it would be, yes.

Q. Well, it does seem to have been Mr Marsh's view; and what exactly did the Governors, when they came to consider this, know about the views of the editor of the programme itself, ie Mr Marsh?

A. Well, they – I do not think the Governors were particularly interested in the editor's view; they were interested in my view; and I shared with them the view I had had for a considerable period of time, and which was certainly partly informed by Mr Marsh and by Mr Mitchell, which was that Andrew Gilligan was in some respects a good reporter. There are two aspects to journalism. There is the finding out of the information and there is then how you present it. My view for some time would be that Andrew Gilligan is extremely good at finding out information but there are sometimes questions of nuance and subtlety in how he presents it which are not all that they should be. Indeed, in my evidence to the Inquiry on August 13th we talked a little bit about some of the issues that arose during his reporting of the Iraq War in that context, and I was frank with the Board of Governors about that, my view of Andrew Gilligan in those terms. I think I described him as a reporter who paints in primary colours rather than something more subtle.

Q. If you had known that Mr Marsh's views were as reflected in this e-mail at the time of the Governor's meeting, would you have thought it right to draw their attention to the fact?

A. I think it is hypothetical because I was not – I did not see this e-mail.

Q. Yes, I know it is hypothetical but I would still like your answer to the question.

A. No, I think the Governors would have wanted to know what my view was.

Q. Right. They would not have been interested in the views of Mr Marsh, as the editor of the programme that was being complained about?

A. Well, only if they significantly differed from mine.

Q. I see. Do you share the views expressed here?

A. I have already told you what my views of Andrew Gilligan's reporting were.

In his evidence Mr Davies said:

[28 August, page 135, line 18]

Q. Can I take you to BBC/5/118, where it was said : ' ...I have to talk to AG [that is Mr Gilligan] early next week. I hope that by then my worst fears ... aren't realised. Assuming not, the guts of what I would say are: 'This story was a good piece of investigative journalism, marred by flawed reporting – our biggest millstone has been his loose use of language and lack of judgment in some of his phraseology.' Also the writing for other outlets and an explanation as to why that might have happened. Did you think you ought to have known of these comments at the Governors' meetings?

A. No, I did not honestly. These comments were between the editor of Today and, I think, the Director of Radio News. They are considerably below the Board of Governors level. What we needed to know at Board of Governors was what the considered judgment of the News Division and the Director General was of Mr Gilligan as a reporter; and these comments do not reflect their considered judgment – I think Mr Sambrook said that in evidence to this Inquiry; and certainly they do not reflect what the Director of News said about Mr Gilligan as a reporter to the Governors.

I am unable to accept these dismissive comments on the relevance and importance of Mr Marsh's e-mail. I consider the lack of knowledge on the part of Mr Sambrook and the Governors of Mr Marsh's e-mail containing criticisms of Mr Gilligan's method of reporting shows a defect in the BBC's management system for the consideration of complaints in respect of broadcasts.

(4)(a) I consider that the Governors found themselves in a difficult position at their meeting on the evening of 6 July as they were being told by the management of the BBC that they were satisfied as to the credibility and reliability of the anonymous source and that Mr Gilligan fully stood by his reports. The view taken by Mr Gavyn Davies is shown in the following passage of his evidence when cross-examined by Mr Sumption:

[24 September, page 30, line 20]

Q. Were you aware that since Mr Gilligan's original broadcast, statements had been made both by Mr Gilligan and himself [Mr Sambrook] that the source was in the Intelligence Services, but that by 6th July Mr Sambrook knew that that was not so?

A. No, I was not aware that – this intelligence source point, Mr Sumption, and the difference between intelligence sources and Intelligence Service sources, had not come across my radar screen in any detail by the time of the Governors' meeting.

Q. Do you not think it should have come across somebody's radar screen if the Governors were going to be properly informed about this?

A. It did come across somebody's radar screen. Both the Director of News and I should imagine the Director General, who broadly knew who the source was, would have thought about it in some detail. I think what Mr Sambrook said to the Inquiry was that when he described the source as an Intelligence Service source on his Today Programme interview, he subsequently realised that that was a mistake but that he did not feel that he could correct that mistake without pointing further fingers at the source. He did not mention any of that to the Governors.

Q. He did not, did he? So the Governors did not know that a part of what had been said about the status of the source on the BBC was known to the Director of News to be wrong; and they had no report on the extent to which Mr Gilligan's notes supported what he had broadcast. Those two points are factually correct, are they not?

A. The Governors did not know anything about the source other than the credibility and reliability of the source as attested by several editors.

Q. In other words, the answer to my question is: no, they did not know either of those two facts and nobody told them.

A. In terms of the notes that Mr Gilligan gave – kept of his meeting with Dr Kelly, the Governors were told that those notes substantiated the broadcast and, more to the point, that Mr Gilligan was standing fully behind his broadcast. Now, I do want to say a word about notes here, because these notes have adopted an extraordinarily large part of the discussions that have been had since. Most journalists broadcast material based, to a large extent, on memory as well as notes; and most journalists do not make verbatim or anywhere near verbatim notes of their discussions. One of the reasons that is the case – and I can tell you this because I have worked, in my career, for a lengthy period of time as a part time journalist – is most journalists think that it puts off the person they are talking to if they either bring out a tape recorder or a notepad. Therefore it is very customary, Mr Sumption, for the journalist's memory to be every bit as important as the journalist's notes.

Q. We know that Mr Gilligan claims that he did, in fact, take notes during his meeting with Dr Kelly. So whatever the general position may be, that does not seem to be a relevant consideration in this case.

A. It does because he has always made it clear that this was not a verbatim set of notes.

Q. Let me take you up on what you said a moment ago, that the Governors were told that Mr Gilligan's notes supported the broadcast. As I understand what you said slightly earlier than that, they were told that even though Mr Sambrook had not examined the notes carefully enough to pick up the point that the 6.07 allegations were not reflected there.

A. As Mr Sambrook correctly told you, at the time the main interest in what the notes said appeared to be in two things: one was whether the notes substantiated *The Mail on Sunday's* article allegation by the source, that the source had used the word 'Campbell' or had attributed to Alastair Campbell the transformation of the document. That was one thing. The second was whether the notes substantiated the 'sexing up' or 'making the document sexier' phrase. And those were the two things that I think Mr Sambrook said were particularly on his mind when he inspected the notes; and the notes did substantiate both those two things.

Q. Was nobody interested in the question whether the notes substantiated the suggestion broadcast by Mr Gilligan that the Government had put material into the dossier knowing that it was probably wrong? Was no one interested in that question?

A. The focus on the 6.07 broadcast, which has become very intense recently in the Government's case, was not actually reflected with the current degree of intensity at the time. Mr Sambrook has said to this Inquiry that it had not acquired the profile, in his thinking, that it has since acquired in the Government's case. I would argue, sir, that it had not acquired this profile in the Government's complaints prior to about the latter part of June either.

Q. I do not accept that, Mr Davies, but I am not going to go through that point with you. That too is a matter of record. But the fact is if Mr Sambrook had carefully gone through the notes and compared them with the transcript of what Mr Gilligan had said, it would have been absolutely apparent to him what all BBC witnesses have acknowledged so far in this Inquiry, namely that Mr Gilligan had gone too far, would it not?

A. He would have noted that the precise words used in the 6.07 broadcast were not duplicated in the notes, and I think he would then have asked Mr Gilligan why; and, in a sense, I would say that actually was – what Mr Gilligan said was that the 6.07 was an interpretation and not a direct quote from the source, he should not have suggested it was a direct quote. It was an interpretation from the source. And he was at that stage standing by it. One of the things I would say about the possibility of a complaints process, and one reason why I think that a full complaints process may have perhaps had problems sorting this particular issue out, is that I think the same thing may have happened. I think they may have looked at the notes, seen that they did not duplicate the words in the 6.07, asked Mr Gilligan why not and Mr Gilligan may well have said: that was a valid interpretation of what the source said to me. That is why I think some further concrete evidence may have been needed to sort this out.

Q. Are you saying that whatever Mr Gilligan said about things that were not in his notes would have been taken at face value by the Governors without further investigation?

A. I did not say anything about the Governors, I was talking about by the PCU.

Q. By the PCU then.

A. I do not think anything would have been taken at face value at all. It would have been taken as evidence, certainly.

...

[24 September, page 36, line 22]

Q. How were the Governors going to form an independent view of the question whether Mr Gilligan had gone further than his source and the question whether the source had been accurately described without having the information before them that was, in fact, in Mr Sambrook's head as this meeting took place?

A. I have already explained to you, I think that the focus on the notes is exaggerated to some degree. And what I think the Governors wanted – I speak for myself, Mr Sumption; what I wanted, as Chairman, was I wanted the considered judgment of the executives that we had appointed to run the news division and the Director General on whether the source was credible and reliable and whether the source was accurately reported. And short of seeking to duplicate their process in a way that would have suggested that we did not trust them, I am not sure what we could have done. Let me explain something to you: the Board of the BBC cannot operate, cannot operate, unless it is in a situation in which it can rely on the good faith and competence of its officers. I am absolutely certain that it can. If it sought to duplicate all of the actions of management it would indeed become the management. There is a gap between what the Board is and does and what the management is and does.

Q. Mr Davies, I quite understand that the Governors' board is a supervisory and, in some respects, an investigatory body. But surely the problem here was that the Governors did in fact duplicate what the executives had done instead of forming a view of their own which, if they had been properly informed, might have been very different?

A. No, they did not duplicate what the executive had done. They expressed the judgment, which I do not resile from at all, that it was in the public interest to put the words of the source into the public domain.

Q. They were put in a position where, for sheer want of information on the point, they had no alternative but to accept the views of the executives although those executives had dug themselves firmly into a position, is that not right?

A. The Governors had a great deal of information going into the meeting and they had an important corroboration for the Gilligan report, which continues to slip out of the mind of the Government; and that is the Susan Watts reports. I said in my first appearance before this Inquiry that the Susan Watts report was not identical to the Gilligan report. I actually studied both before I went into the meeting and I knew they were not identical, but I equally knew that the burden of what Mr Gilligan had reported in his many broadcasts on the subject at the end of May was a close match to the burden of what Ms Watts reported on 2nd and 4th June. And I do not think it should be forgotten that that is the case, because certainly in my mind, and in several other Governors' mind, maybe the whole of the Board of Governors who received the information before they went into the meeting, that was seen as an important corroboration of the Gilligan story.

Q. Would you turn to BBC/6/107, please? This is part of the official minute of the meeting in question. After the executives are drawn it says, second paragraph from the top of the page: 'Following an account from Mark Damazer about how the '45 minutes claim' had been disputed by the Government since the broadcast, and a discussion by Governors about the accuracy of the report, Gavyn Davies reminded the Board that it was not a matter for them.' So is the position that when the Governors did start discussing the accuracy of the report you intervened to stop them?

A. I think that is a very tendentious way of putting it. I was reminding them, as I had said to them in the e-mail on the Friday and had basically been agreed with by all Governors, that the intrinsic accuracy of the report, ie whether the source was telling, fundamentally, the truth or not, as opposed to whether we were accurately reporting him, was something that we were not in a position to determine. I therefore felt at this stage, and other Governors agreed with me, that the discussion was interesting but going down a by-way which we could not reach a conclusion on.

Q. I see. You could not, of course, without the information.

A. No, we could not have got the information, Mr Sumption. There was no way of obtaining the information.

(4)(b) The Governors were right to take the view that it was their duty to protect the independence of the BBC against attacks by the Government and there is no doubt that Mr Campbell's complaints were being expressed in exceptionally strong terms which raised very considerably the temperature of the dispute between the Government and the BBC, but Mr Campbell's allegation that the BBC had an anti-war agenda in his evidence to the FAC was only one part of his evidence. The Government's concern about Mr Gilligan's broadcast on the 29 May was a separate issue about which specific complaints had been made by the Government. Therefore I consider that the Governors should have recognised more fully than they did that their duty to protect the independence of the BBC was not incompatible with giving proper consideration to whether there was validity in the Government's complaints, no matter how strongly worded by Mr Campbell, that the allegations against its integrity reported in Mr Gilligan's broadcasts were unfounded and the Governors failed to give this issue proper consideration. The view taken by the Governors, as explained by Mr Gavyn Davies in his evidence, that they had to rely on the BBC management to investigate and assess whether Mr Gilligan's source was reliable and credible and that it was not for them as Governors to investigate whether the allegations reported were themselves accurate, is a view which is understandable. However I consider that this was not the correct view for the Governors to take because the Government had stated to the BBC in clear terms, as had Mr Campbell to the FAC, that the report that the Government probably knew that the 45 minutes claim was wrong was untruthful, and this denial was made with the authority of the Prime Minister and the Chairman of the JIC. In those circumstances, rather than relying on the assurances of BBC management, I consider that the Governors themselves should have made more detailed investigations into the extent to which Mr Gilligan's notes supported his report. If they had done this they would probably have discovered that the notes did not support the allegation that the Government knew that the 45 minutes claim was probably wrong, and the Governors should then have questioned whether it was right for the BBC to maintain that it was in the public interest to broadcast that allegation in Mr Gilligan's report from an anonymous source and to rely on Mr Gilligan's assurance that his report was accurate. Therefore in the very unusual and specific circumstances relating to Mr Gilligan's broadcasts, I consider that the Governors are to be criticised for themselves failing to make more detailed investigations into whether this allegation reported by Mr Gilligan was properly supported by his notes and for failing to give proper and adequate consideration to whether the BBC should publicly acknowledge that this very grave allegation should not have been broadcast.

Summary of conclusions relating to the BBC arising from Mr Gilligan's broadcasts on the BBC Today programme on 29 May 2003

The allegations reported by Mr Gilligan on the BBC Today programme on 29 May 2003 that the Government probably knew that the 45 minutes claim was wrong or questionable before the dossier was published and that it was not inserted in the first draft of the dossier because it only came from one source and the intelligence agencies did not really believe it was necessarily true, were unfounded.

The communication by the media of information (including information obtained by investigative reporters) on matters of public interest and importance is a vital part of life in a democratic society. However the right to communicate such information is subject to the qualification (which itself exists for the benefit of a democratic society) that false accusations of fact impugning the integrity of others, including politicians, should not be made by the media. Where a reporter is intending to broadcast or publish information impugning the integrity of others the management of his broadcasting company or newspaper should ensure that a system is in place whereby his editor or editors give careful consideration to the wording of the report and to whether it is right in all the circumstances to broadcast or publish it. The allegations that Mr Gilligan was intending to broadcast in respect of the Government and the preparation of the dossier were very grave allegations in relation to a subject of great importance and I consider that the editorial system which the BBC permitted was defective in that Mr Gilligan was allowed to broadcast his report at 6.07am without editors having seen a script of what he was going to say and having considered whether it should be approved.

The BBC management was at fault in the following respects in failing to investigate properly the Government's complaints that the report in the 6.07am broadcast was false that the Government probably knew that the 45 minutes claim was wrong even before it decided to put it in the dossier. The BBC management failed, before Mr Sambrook wrote his letter of 27 June 2003 to Mr Campbell, to make an examination of Mr Gilligan's notes on his personal organiser of his meeting with Dr Kelly to see if they supported the allegations which he had reported in his broadcast at 6.07am. When the BBC management did look at Mr Gilligan's notes after 27 June it failed to appreciate that the notes did not fully support the most serious of the allegations which he had reported in the 6.07am broadcast, and it therefore failed to draw the attention of the Governors to the lack of support in the notes for the most serious of the allegations.

The e-mail sent by Mr Kevin Marsh, the editor of the Today programme on 27 June 2003 to Mr Stephen Mitchell, the Head of Radio News, (see paragraph 284) which was critical of Mr Gilligan's method of reporting, and which referred to Mr Gilligan's 'loose use of language and lack of judgment in some of his phraseology' and referred also to 'the loose and in some ways distant relationship he's been allowed to have with Today,' was clearly relevant to the complaints which the Government were making about his broadcasts on 29 May, and the lack of knowledge on the part of Mr Sambrook, the Director of News and the Governors of this critical e-mail shows a defect in the operation of the BBC's management system for the consideration of complaints in respect of broadcasts.

Issues relating to the decisions and actions taken by the Government after Dr Kelly informed his line manager in the MoD that he had spoken to Mr Gilligan on 22 May 2003

These issues are the following:

(a) Did the Government behave in a way which was dishonourable or under-hand or duplicitous in revealing Dr Kelly's name to the media, thereby subjecting him to the pressure and stress which were bound to arise from being placed in the media spotlight?

(b) If the Government did not behave in a way which was dishonourable or underhand or duplicitous in revealing Dr Kelly's name to the media, did the Government fail to take proper steps to help and protect Dr Kelly in the difficult position in which he found himself?

Conclusion on the issue whether the Government behaved in a way which was dishonourable or underhand or duplicitous in revealing Dr Kelly's name to the media

My conclusion is that there was no dishonourable or underhand or duplicitous strategy by the Government covertly to leak Dr Kelly's name to the media. If the bare details of the MoD statement dated 8 July 2003, the changing drafts of the Q and A material prepared in the MoD, and the lobby briefings by the Prime Minister's official spokesman on 9 July are looked at in isolation from the surrounding circumstances it would be possible to infer, as some commentators have done, that there was an underhand strategy by the Government to leak Dr Kelly's name in a covert way. However having heard a large volume of evidence on this issue I have concluded that there was no such strategy on the part of the Government. I consider that in the midst of a major controversy relating to Mr Gilligan's broadcasts which had contained very grave allegations against the integrity of the Government and fearing that Dr Kelly's name as the source for those broadcasts would be disclosed by the media at any time, the Government's main concern was that it would be charged with a serious cover up if it did not reveal that a civil servant had come forward. I consider that the evidence of Mr Donald Anderson MP and Mr Andrew Mackinlay MP, the Chairman and a member respectively of the FAC, together with the questions put by Sir John Stanley MP to Dr Kelly when he appeared before the FAC, clearly show that the Government's concern was well founded. Therefore I consider that the Government did not behave in a dishonourable or underhand or duplicitous way in issuing on 8 July, after it had been read over to Dr Kelly and he had said that he was content with it, a statement which said that a civil servant, who was not named, had come forward to volunteer that he had met Mr Gilligan on 22 May.

I further consider that the decision by the MoD to confirm Dr Kelly's name if, after the statement had been issued, the correct name were put to the MoD by a reporter, was not part of a covert strategy to leak his name, but was based on the view that in a matter of such intense public and media interest it would not be sensible to try to conceal the name when the MoD thought that the press were bound to discover the correct name, and a further consideration in the mind of the MoD was that it did not think it right that media speculation should focus, wrongly, on other civil servants.

In addition I consider that it was reasonable for the Government to take the view that, even if it sought to keep confidential the fact that Dr Kelly had come forward, the controversy surrounding Mr Gilligan's broadcasts was so great and the level of media interest was so intense that Dr Kelly's name as Mr Gilligan's source was bound to become known to the public and that it was not a practical possibility to keep his name secret.


Consideration of the issue whether the Government failed to take proper steps to help and protect Dr Kelly in the difficult position in which he found himself

The evidence has satisfied me that officials in the MoD did give some consideration to Dr Kelly's welfare and did take some steps to help him.

It is apparent from the evidence that Sir Kevin Tebbit gave thought to Dr Kelly's welfare. In his minute of 10 July 2003 to Mr Hoon he recommended that Mr Hoon should resist Dr Kelly appearing before the FAC when he was going to appear before the ISC, and he wrote:

A further reason for avoiding two hearings, back to back, is to show some regard for the man himself. He has come forward voluntarily, is not used to being thrust into the public eye, and is not on trial. It does not seem unreasonable to ask the FAC to show restraint and accept the [ISC] hearing as being sufficient for their purposes (eg testing the validity of Gilligan's evidence).

However it would not have been possible for Mr Hoon to refuse to permit Dr Kelly to appear before the ISC as it is the Committee directly responsible for investigating intelligence matters. I also consider that the evidence of Mr Donald Anderson MP and Mr Andrew Mackinlay MP shows that there would have been a serious political storm if Mr Hoon had refused to permit Dr Kelly to appear before the FAC and that Mr Hoon's decision not to accept Sir Kevin Tebbit's advice and to agree to Dr Kelly appearing before the FAC is not a decision which can be subject to valid criticism.

Sir Kevin Tebbit also enquired from other officials how Dr Kelly was bearing up under the stress and he was told that Dr Kelly was handling the pressure pretty well. There is a minute from Mr Colin Smith of the FCO to another official in the FCO dated 14 July 2003 referring to a meeting which he had attended that morning on Iraq's WMD and which also had been attended by Mr Martin Howard. In the minute Mr Smith stated 'Kelly is apparently feeling the pressure, and does not appear to be handling it well'. In his evidence Mr Howard said that he did not recall saying that, and if he did, it would purely have been passing on a second hand account of what might have been said to him because he had not seen Dr Kelly since his meeting with him and Mr Hatfield on 7 July. Mr Howard said that at the end of the meeting with Dr Kelly on the afternoon of 14 July Dr Kelly was composed, obviously nervous, which was to be expected, but he saw no evidence to show that he was not ready for the meeting. When Dr Wells was asked by Mr Gompertz whether he thought that some form of professional counselling would have been a good idea Dr Wells replied:

> A. David was an experienced civil servant; he had experience of stressful situations as a UN weapons inspector. In answer to repeated questions, he said he was tired but otherwise fine. And I have to say when someone of that seniority and experience repeatedly assures me that he is fine, then I am bound to take him at his word.

The assessment of how a person under stress is reacting can be a somewhat subjective one which depends to some extent on the person making it, and I think that different people may have formed different impressions as to how Dr Kelly was reacting to the strain. Dr Kelly's daughter, Rachel, who was very close to her father, knew that he was under great strain but her fiancé, Mr David Wilkins said that on Sunday night, 13 July, and on the morning and evening of Monday 14 July, he did not seem overly agitated or under stress and seemed 'okay', although at supper on Tuesday evening, 15 July, after he had appeared before the FAC he seemed to be very withdrawn within himself and it was noticeable that he was going through some personal trauma. Therefore I think it was reasonable for Sir Kevin Tebbit to take the view, which he described in evidence, that Dr Kelly was an experienced and robust individual who had dealt well with stressful and difficult situations in Iraq.

As I have stated, I am satisfied that Mr Hatfield was not engaged in any 'plea bargain' strategy when he conducted his meetings with Dr Kelly on 4 and 7 July, and I think his notes dated 7 and 8 July of meetings show that he dealt with Dr Kelly in a way which was fair to him.

On the afternoon of 8 July after Mr Hatfield had read over on the telephone to Dr Kelly the new draft of the MoD press statement, Mr Hatfield advised him that he should talk to the press office and to Dr Wells about support.

On the evening of 8 July between 8pm and 9pm after the MoD statement had been issued Mrs Kate Wilson, the chief press officer in the MoD, having agreed to do so in a discussion with Ms Pamela Teare, the Director of News in the MoD, telephoned Dr Kelly and told him that the statement had been put out, that the press office had had a lot of follow up questions and that he needed to think about alternative accommodation. Mrs Wilson asked Dr Kelly if there was anything he wanted from her and he said there was not.

I am satisfied that Dr Wells, who liked and admired Dr Kelly, tried to help and support him after the MoD statement was issued on 8 July. Dr Wells telephoned Dr Kelly when he was in the West Country from 10 to 13 July to arrange his appearances before the FAC and the ISC, but he also called him to check that he was bearing up under the stress of press interest. In addition Dr Wells had arranged to attend a meeting in New York during the first part of the week commencing Monday 14 July, but he cancelled his visit to New York in order to be in London to give support to Dr Kelly and he told Dr Kelly that he was doing this. Dr Wells also offered Dr Kelly hotel accommodation in London on the night of Monday 14 July to save him from travelling up and down to London from his home in Oxfordshire, but Dr Kelly said that he wished to stay with his daughter in Oxford.

When Dr Kelly went to give evidence before the FAC on Tuesday 15 July Dr Wells and Wing Commander Clark, who was a friend and colleague of Dr Kelly in the MoD, accompanied him in order to give him moral support and sat behind him during the hearing. They were also accompanied by Mrs Wilson who was present to give Dr Kelly assistance if the press tried to interview him. Dr Wells and Wing Commander Clark also accompanied Dr Kelly when he gave evidence in private before the ISC on Wednesday 16 July.

The issue was raised in the course of the Inquiry whether an official of the MoD should have sat, not behind, but beside Dr Kelly at the table to give him support when he was questioned by the FAC. Dr Wells gave evidence that when he was in the West Country Dr Kelly told him on the telephone that he would like a colleague to accompany him to the FAC because he was uncertain about procedures. Therefore when Mr Hoon wrote to the Chairman of the FAC, Mr Donald Anderson, on 11 July, he said in the course of the letter: 'As he is not used to this degree of public exposure, Dr Kelly has asked if he could be accompanied by a colleague. MoD officials will discuss this further with the Clerk.' However when Dr Wells discussed this point with the Clerk of the FAC on the morning of Monday 14 July the Clerk told him that if a colleague sat beside Dr Kelly at the table it would be open to the FAC to ask questions of the colleague. In his evidence Dr Wells said that when he and Mr Martin Howard met Dr Kelly in the afternoon of Monday 14 July he raised with him the matter of a colleague sitting beside him, and it was implicit in Dr Wells' evidence that he told Dr Kelly about the point made by the Clerk of the

FAC. At the end of the meeting after the discussion about the likely areas of questioning by the FAC and the ISC and about how the two Committees were differently constituted, Dr Wells asked Dr Kelly how he felt about having a colleague next to him at the table and Dr Kelly said that as he now had a good understanding of the procedures and the likely areas of questioning he no longer felt the need to have a colleague sitting beside him. I think it is probable that if a colleague had been sitting beside him this would have given Dr Kelly a feeling of support, particularly when he was questioned in a forceful way by one member of the Committee. But looking at the situation as it presented itself to the MoD before the hearing, I think it is understandable that the MoD decided not to have an official sitting beside Dr Kelly. First, because Dr Kelly was being called as a witness, not to state an official line, but to state his own personal involvement in having an unauthorised meeting with Mr Gilligan and, secondly, because a colleague sitting beside Dr Kelly might have been regarded as an official 'minder' who was sitting beside Dr Kelly to inhibit him in the expression of his own views relating to WMD.

Therefore I am satisfied that some efforts were made by officials in the MoD to give help and support to Dr Kelly. Mrs Kelly and Miss Rachel Kelly's fiancé, Mr David Wilkins, gave evidence as to Dr Kelly's view of the support he was receiving. Mrs Kelly said:

Q. Did you speak to him at all on the Monday [14th July]?

A. Yes, I did. After he had returned to Rachel's he rang me to say that the day had not been too tormenting. He was not worried about what had gone on by that day. I asked if he was being supported by the MoD and he said: I suppose so, yes. He always previously said yes when I asked this question on several occasions before, so he was a little bit less certain, I felt.

I was a bit worried about the lack of support or the lack of apparent support. He was not an easy man to support in some ways, he would always try to give the impression that he was okay, and I think his immediate line manager was a much younger man than him and he would have tried, as he did with us, to protect him from his own feelings. He tried to keep his feelings to himself.

Mr David Wilkins said, referring to Wednesday 16 July:

Q. And did he comment about the support or absence of support he was getting?

A. Yes, he did. He said that his colleagues – he said that colleagues had been 'tremendously supportive', that is a direct quote. I remember him saying that, that they had been tremendously supportive. I did get the impression that it was not all colleagues. I cannot remember his exact wording, but the implication and the impression I was left with was that it was some but not all.

However, notwithstanding that steps were taken by a number of officials to give support to Dr Kelly and despite the fact that Dr Kelly was told expressly by Mrs Wilson, the chief press officer at the MoD, in a telephone conversation on the evening of 8 July that he needed to think about staying with friends, which would have conveyed to him that he could be the subject of intense press interest, and although it is clear from remarks which he made to Mrs Kelly (see paragraph 400) and to Ms Olivia Bosch (see paragraph 401) that Dr Kelly realised that his name would come out, I consider (without engaging in hindsight) that the MoD was at fault in the procedure which it adopted in relation to Dr Kelly after the decision had been taken to release the statement which was issued about 5.30pm on Tuesday 8 July. The principal fault lay in the failure of the MoD to inform Dr Kelly that the press office was going to confirm his name if a journalist suggested it. It would have been a better course if (1) the MoD had decided to name Dr Kelly with his consent in the statement it issued; (2) the MoD had told Dr Kelly in a face to face meeting with an official or officials that this was its intention and had obtained his consent to this course; and (3) the MoD had delayed issuing a statement for a period of, perhaps, twenty-four hours, to give adequate time for the press office to give Dr Kelly advice about the intense press interest to which he would be subject and for him to consider whether he wished to move to alternative accommodation to avoid press intrusion or, if he did not, for the press office to have a press officer in position at his home to deal with members of the press. In his evidence Mr Campbell recognised that this would have been a better course to adopt and he said:

A .... But I think again, and I emphasise this is with an element of hindsight, that probably what I feel I maybe should have expressed more forcefully at that time is: look, if you are in this kind of situation you do have to have some element of control over the process here. You cannot just let this sort of dribble out in a way that you are not clear how it is then going to unfold. So I think the desired outcome, given that everybody, including it seems Dr Kelly, understood that it is likely because of the importance of this development he was likely to be identified, he was likely to have to appear at one or both Select Committees, far better it would have been for that to be announced properly, cleanly, straightforwardly and then you can actually put in place all the proper support that somebody who is not used to this kind of pressure can then maybe better deal with.

However because of its concern that the press might become aware of, and publish, Dr Kelly's name at any moment and it would then be charged with a cover up, the Government did not follow this course but decided on Tuesday 8 July that a statement should be issued without delay that a civil servant had come forward without naming the civil servant. For the reasons which I have given, I consider that the Government's concern was justifiable and that it should not be criticised for underhand or dishonourable or duplicitous conduct in issuing the statement without naming Dr Kelly once it was reasonably satisfied, without being certain, that he was Mr Gilligan's source.

But once the decision had been taken to issue the statement I consider that the MoD was at fault in two respects. The principal fault lay, as I have stated, in not telling Dr Kelly that the press office would confirm his name if a journalist suggested it. Although I am satisfied that Dr Kelly realised, once the statement had been issued, that his name would come out, and although he had been told by Mrs Wilson on the previous evening that he should consider staying with friends, it must have been a great shock for him to learn in a brief telephone call from Dr Wells that the press office of his own department had confirmed his name to the press, and to discover this at about the same time as Mr Rufford told him that the press were on their way in droves, and in consequence he made a very hurried departure from his home.

In her evidence Mrs Kelly said that Dr Kelly felt betrayed by the MoD because he told her that he had received assurances from it that his name would not go into the public domain:

Q. Had you spoken with Dr Kelly at all during the day [Wednesday 9th July] about his reaction to the news the night before?

A. Yes, I had. He said several times over coffee, over lunch, over afternoon tea that he felt totally let down and betrayed. It seemed to me that this was all part of what might have happened anyway because it seemed to have been a very loose arrangement with the MoD, they did not seem to take a lot of account of his time. There was a lot of wasting of his time. I just felt that this must have been very frustrating for him. David often said: they are not using me properly. He felt that the MoD were not quite sure how to use his expertise at times, although I have later seen his manager's reports on his staff appraisals where he obviously did warrant his or respect his expertise. But that is not the impression that I got.

Q. You say, I think, that he had felt totally let down and betrayed. Who did he say that of?

A. He did not say in so many terms but I believed he meant the MoD because they were the ones that had effectively let his name be known in the public domain.

Q. And did you get the impression that he was happy or unhappy that this press statement had been made?

A. Well, he did not know about it until after it had happened. So he was – I think initially he had been led to believe that it would not go into the public domain. He had received assurances and that is why he was so very upset about it.

Q. What, he did not know that the press statement saying an unnamed source had come forward would be made?

A. Not until after the event.

LORD HUTTON: Did he say from whom he had received assurances Mrs Kelly?

A. From his line manager, from all their seniors and from the people he had been interviewed by.

MR DINGEMANS: And his reaction on hearing the news, you said he had seemed slightly reluctant to watch the news that night.

A. Yes, indeed.

Q. Was that because he had seen an earlier news, do you think, or because he knew something might be coming up?

A. I think it was probably trepidation that this was the moment. He was not quite sure when it would actually happen but since Nick had come it was going to be a big problem. He knew that.

I am satisfied that Dr Kelly had been told by the MoD that his name would probably come out and that he realised this himself, as is shown by his telephone conversation with Ms Olivia Bosch, and I am also satisfied that he knew that the MoD was going to issue a statement that a civil servant had come forward and that the text of the statement was read over to him on the telephone by Mr Hatfield on the afternoon of 8 July and that he said that he was content with it. However the sudden information from Dr Wells that his name had

to elapse between the confirmation of his name to the press and information being given to Dr Kelly that his name had been confirmed to the press. However these criticisms are subject to the mitigating circumstances that (1) Dr Kelly's exposure to press attention and intrusion, whilst obviously very stressful, was only one of the factors placing him under great stress; (2) individual officials in the MoD did try to help and support him in the ways which I have described (3) because of his intensely private nature, Dr Kelly was not an easy man to help or to whom to give advice.

On the issue of the factors which may have led Dr Kelly to take his own life I adopt as my own conclusion the opinion which Professor Hawton, the Professor of Psychiatry at Oxford University, expressed in the course of his evidence:

Q. Have you considered, now, with the benefit of hindsight that we all have, what factors did contribute to Dr Kelly's death?

A. I think that as far as one can deduce, the major factor was the severe loss of self esteem, resulting from his feeling that people had lost trust in him and from his dismay at being exposed to the media.

Q. And why have you singled that out as a major factor?

A. Well, he talked a lot about it; and I think being such a private man, I think this was anathema to him to be exposed, you know, publicly in this way. In a sense, I think he would have seen it as being publicly disgraced.

Q. What other factors do you think were relevant?

A. Well, I think that carrying on that theme, I think that he must have begun – he is likely to have begun to think that, first of all, the prospects for continuing in his previous work role were diminishing very markedly and, indeed, my conjecture that he had begun to fear he would lose his job altogether.

Q. What effect is that likely to have had on him?

A. Well, I think that would have filled him with a profound sense of hopelessness; and that, in a sense, his life's work had been not wasted but that had been totally undermined.

LORD HUTTON: Could you just elaborate a little on that, Professor, again? As sometimes is the case in this Inquiry, witnesses give answers and further explanation is obvious, but nonetheless I think it is helpful just to have matters fully spelt out. What do you think would have caused Dr Kelly to think that the prospects of continuing in his work were becoming uncertain?

A. Well, I think, my Lord, that first of all, there had been the letter from Mr Hatfield which had laid out the difficulties that Dr Kelly, you know, is alleged to have got into.

LORD HUTTON: Yes.

A. And in that letter there was also talk that should further matters come to light then disciplinary proceedings would need to be instigated.

LORD HUTTON: Yes.

A. And then of course there were the Parliamentary Questions which we have heard about, which suggested that questions were going to be asked about discipline in Parliament.

LORD HUTTON: Yes. Thank you.

MR DINGEMANS: Were there any other relevant factors?

A. I think the fact that he could not share his problems and feelings with other people, and the fact that he, according to the accounts I have been given, actually increasingly withdrew into himself. So in a sense he was getting further and further from being able to share the problems with other people, that is extremely important.

Q. Were there any other factors which you considered relevant?

A. Those are the main factors that I consider relevant.

# CHAPTER 7

I wish to record my gratitude and thanks to Mrs Kelly and her daughters for the great assistance which they have given to the Inquiry in a time of great sorrow and stress for them.

Dr Kelly was a devoted husband and father and a public servant who served his country and the international community with great distinction both in the United Kingdom and in very difficult and testing conditions in Russia and Iraq. The evidence at this Inquiry has concentrated largely on the last two months of Dr Kelly's life, and therefore it is fitting that I should end this report with some words written in Dr Kelly's obituary in *The Independent* on 31 July by Mr Terence Taylor, the President and Executive Director of the International Institute of Strategic Studies, Washington DC and a former colleague of Dr Kelly:

> 'It is most important that the extraordinary public attention and political fallout arising from the events of the past month do not mask the extraordinary achievements of a scientist who loyally served not only his Government but also the international community at large.'

Brian Hutton<br>28 January 2004

# Tim Coates

**Crime**
The Great British Train Robbery, 1963 (Illustrated)
Rillington Place, 1949
The Strange Story of Adolf Beck
The Trials of Oscar Wilde, 1895

**Ireland**
Bloody Sunday: Lord Widgery's report, 1972
The Irish Book of Death and Flying Ships (Illustrated)
The Irish Uprising, 1914–21
The Theft of the Irish Crown Jewels: the unsolved mystery (Illustrated, 2004)

**Transport**
The Loss of the Titanic, 1912
R.101: the airship disaster, 1930
Tragic Journeys (Titanic, R.101, Munich Air Crash)

**Travel and British Empire**
The Amritsar Massacre: General Dyer in the Punjab, 1919
The Boer War: Ladysmith and Mafeking, 1900
The British Invasion of Tibet: Colonel Younghusband, 1904
The British War in Afghanistan: the dreadful retreat from Kabul in 1842 (Illustrated, 2004)
Florence Nightingale and the Crimea, 1854–55
King Guezo of Dahomey, 1850–52
Mr Hosie's Journey to Tibet, 1904

Peace in Tibet: the Younghusband expedition, 1904 (Illustrated, 2004)
The Siege Collection (Kars, Boer War, Peking)
The Siege of Kars, 1855
The Siege of the Peking Embassy, 1900
Travels in Mongolia, 1902
Wilfrid Blunt's Egyptian Garden: fox–hunting in Cairo

## Tudor history
Letters of Henry VIII, 1526–29

## UK politics since 1945
The Hutton Inquiry, 2003
John Profumo and Christine Keeler, 1963
The Scandal of Christine Keeler and John Profumo. Lord Denning's
    report (Illustrated)
UFOs in the House of Lords, 1979
War in the Falklands, 1982

## United States of America
The Assassination of John F. Kennedy, 1963
The Cuban Missile Crisis, 1962
John Lennon: the FBI files (Illustrated)
Marilyn Monroe: the FBI files (Illustrated)
Nixon and Watergate: the Watergate Special Prosecution report
    (Illustrated, 2004)
Sacco and Vanzetti: the FBI files (Illustrated, 2004)
The St Valentine's Day Massacre, 1929
The Shooting of John F. Kennedy, 1963 (Illustrated, 2004)
UFOs in America, 1947
The Watergate Affair, 1972

## World War I
British Battles of World War I, 1914–15
Defeat at Gallipoli: the Dardanelles Commission Part II, 1915–16

Lord Kitchener and Winston Churchill: the Dardanelles Commission Part
 I, 1914–15
The Russian Revolution, 1917
War 1914: punishing the Serbs
The World War I Collection (Dardanelles Commission, British Battles of
 World War I)
Worldwide Battles of the Great War, 1914–1916

## World War II

Attack on Pearl Harbor, 1941
D Day to VE Day: General Eisenhower's report, 1944–45
Escape from Germany, 1939–45
Escaping from Germany: the British government files (Illustrated, 2004)
The Judgment of Nuremberg, 1946
Tragedy at Bethnal Green
Victory in Europe, 1944–1945: General Eisenhower's report (Illustrated,
 2004)
War 1939: dealing with Adolf Hitler
War in Italy, 1944: the battles for Monte Cassino (Illustrated, 2004)
The World War II Collection (War 1939, D Day to VE Day, Judgment
 of Nuremberg)

## World War II facsimiles

*(Illustrated books published by the British government during the war years)*
The Battle of Britain, August–October 1940
The Battle of Egypt, 1942
Bomber Command, September 1939–July 1941
East of Malta, West of Suez, September 1939 to March 1941
Fleet Air Arm, 1943
The Highland Division by Eric Linklater (2004)
Land at War, 1939–1944
The Mediterranean Fleet: Greece to Tripoli (2004)
Ocean Front: the story of the war in the Pacific, 1941–1944
Roof over Britain, 1939–1942

## UK Distribution and Orders

Littlehampton Book Services, Faraday Close, Durrington, West Sussex BN13 3RB
Telephone: 01903 828800  Fax: 01903 828801
E–mail: orders@lbsltd.co.uk

## Sales Representation

Compass Independent Book Sales, Barley Mow Centre, 10 Barley Mow Passage,
Chiswick, London W4 4PH
Telephone: 0208 994 6477  Fax: 0208 400 6132

## US Sales and Distribution

Midpoint Trade Books, 27 West 20th Street, Suite 1102, New York, NY 10011
Telephone: (1) 212 727 0190  Fax: (1) 212 727 0195

Midpoint Trade Books, 1263 Southwest Blvd, Kansas City, KS 66103
Telephone: (1) 913 831 2233  Fax: (1) 913 362 7401

## Other Representation
## Australia

Nick Walker, Australian Book Marketing/Australian Scholarly Publishing Pty Ltd
PO Box 299, Kew, Victoria 3101; Suite 102, 282 Collins Street, Melbourne 3000
Telephone: 03 9654 0250  Fax: 03 9663 0161
E–mail: aspec@ozemail.com.au

## Scandinavia

Hanne Rotovnik, Publishers' Representative, Taarbaek, PO Box 5, Strandvej 59 0,
DK–2930 Klampenborg
E–mail: Hanne@rotovnik.dk

## South Africa

Colin McGee, Stephan Phillips (Pty) Ltd, PO Box 434, Umdloti Beach 4350
Telephone: +27 (0) 31 568 2902  Fax: +27 (0) 31 568 2922
E–mail: colinmcgee@mweb.co.za

Titles can also be ordered from www.timcoatesbooks.com.